On the Deck or In the Drink

On the Deck or In the Drink

Flying with the Royal Navy
1952–1964

Lieutenant B.R. Allen RN Rtd.

Pen & Sword
AVIATION

First published in Great Britain in 2010 by
Pen & Sword Aviation
an imprint of
Pen & Sword Books Ltd
47 Church Street
Barnsley
South Yorkshire
S70 2AS

ISBN 978 1 84884 189 5

A CIP catalogue record for this book is available from the British Library.

Printed and bound in England
by CPI.

Pen & Sword Books Ltd incorporates the imprints of
Pen & Sword Aviation, Pen & Sword Maritime, Pen & Sword Military,
Wharncliffe Local History, Pen & Sword Select, Pen & Sword Military Classics,
Leo Cooper, Remember When, Seaforth Publishing and Frontline Publishing.

For a complete list of Pen & Sword titles please contact
PEN & SWORD BOOKS LIMITED
47 Church Street, Barnsley, South Yorkshire, S70 2AS, England
E-mail: enquiries@pen-and-sword.co.uk
Website: www.pen-and-sword.co.uk

Contents

Introduction and Acknowledgements   vii

Chapter 1   Every Story has a Beginning   1

Chapter 2   Rise and Shine, Young Sirs!   23

Chapter 3   A Sailor's Life for Me   35

Chapter 4   'I Have Control'   45

Chapter 5   Onwards and Upwards   55

Chapter 6   You are Commanded to Proceed   67

Chapter 7   Here Come the Big, Fat Faireys   73

Chapter 8   825 Squadron – The First Commission   79

Chapter 9   751 Squadron and HMS *Warrior*   95

Chapter 10   What are you doing at Christmas? Operation Grapple   101

Chapter 11   One Elderly Aircraft Carrier for Sale   121

Chapter 12   The Ups and Downs of a Rotary Wing Pilot   129

Chapter 13   Off Again – 815 Squadron   147

Chapter 14   Trials and Development – Whatever Next?   161

Chapter 15   A Tragic Conclusion   171

Chapter 16   Someone Has to Do It   177

Appendix   183

Index   185

Introduction and Acknowledgements

Having reached the doddery old age of 76, nearly everything that has happened in my life is a nostalgic memory, sometimes good, often bad. Wandering along memory lane is an old boy's indulgence. As my old naval friend Tony Wilson keeps telling me, 'You should get it down in print, or it's lost forever'. Other friends, after laughing at the odd anecdote, have said, 'You should put it in a book,' so here it is.

My twelve years' service in the Fleet Air Arm was one of the more colourful parts of my life and, I have to confess, it seems that I didn't appreciate those days as much as I should have done. One of the failures of youth is that we live for the day without savouring the event. We are too young to appreciate the present and have too little of the past to worry about. I was fortunate to have a naval career that was an adventure in itself.

I served as a front line pilot, as most do who join the Fleet Air Arm as I did, but had the chance to partake in some of the more specialized duties in small units with unique tasks to carry out. Many of my friends from those halcyon days failed to survive; others have passed on through more natural causes. This makes me even more aware of my own good fortune and they were all certainly in my thoughts as I wrote these words.

I should perhaps explain the titling of this saga. A naval flier normally has two choices open to him on returning to the carrier. A successful landing, often jokingly referred to as a 'controlled crash' will end with the aircraft safely on the deck. Failure will result in the aircraft ending up in the sea, hopefully, with a measure of good luck, safely. The somewhat nonchalant slang used by aircrew, usually referred to such an immersion as ending up 'in the drink'. For a while I held the unenviable record for 'ditching', not, I hasten to add, through any fault of mine.

Having been long retired, I must apologize in advance if any of the traditional Royal Navy language slips into the text. It is a strange tongue culled from mariners over the centuries and fragments seem to stay with one forever. I often lapse inadvertently, declaring that someone has 'gone ashore', or only served a 'dogwatch' when in fact they have gone out or been with one for only a short time. The lapses are largely understood, and forgiven by naval friends and their long suffering wives but the normal listener is prone to give a blank stare. I promise I will try to write in acceptable prose. Like all memoirs, they are my personal memories of incidents in my life that have remained with me for seventy or so years; I must admit that my version may not always coincide with that of someone who shared the event. Some things, as in political life, have been 'massaged' to make the reading more interesting. It does, however, record pretty accurately the adventures of a middle class, suburban boy who ended up flying multi-million pound aircraft for the 'senior service', on some unusual commissions, and equally unusual experiences.

I would like to record my undying love and appreciation to my ever loyal, supportive wife, Pat. She, like so many naval wives, spent a great deal of time alone and coping with the 'pack and follow' nomadic life of the naval family. After the birth of our son, she had the additional concerns of bringing up a small child, often alone, in the same environment. Whilst I readily admit that all service families deal with such 'exigencies of the Service', they are not the normal domestic routines of civilian life. She reminisced recently, that in twenty years' of Service life she had packed and made a new home in twenty-two changes of accommodation. Although rarely mentioned, she and my son are the main reason for this personal history of what, for me, was a fascinating and happy time. Amazingly, my wife also agrees that she too loved the experience.

I must also record my debt to Tony Wilson for his invaluable help with this book. His own unpublished work, a whole life story for his immediate family to appreciate at a future date, sowed the seed and his help and advice, often uncharitably called 'nitpicking', kept me well counselled. We shared a cabin with our two observers in HMS *Albion* during her 1960 Far East voyage, having met briefly in 1955 in the Search and Rescue Flight at RNAS Eglinton. As often happens we went our separate ways in the Service and lost contact until, after a gap of forty years, whilst reading the 'Lost and Found' column in the *Daily Mail*, I found he had retired to Devon. I managed to track him down and our friendship has been re-established in recent years. To the well observed boredom of our wives we repeatedly recount our tales of 'derring do' in aircraft that are now found only in museums – as we should be – to anyone who will listen.

As in every career, mine had its moments of joy and sorrow, comedy and tragedy, frantic activity and acute boredom. Unlike most careers it involved a great deal of moving from location to location. From air station to ship, from course to course, and by the nature of the job, one part of the world to another. I knew this and accepted it as all part of the great adventure. Wives and families had no choice but to follow, or stay in one place and live a fragmented family life.

Life as a naval officer is also very different to that of the society that I came from, and I am certain I was not alone in finding that it was not always easy in meeting the criteria that had been developed, often over centuries. Of necessity, the disciplines in the Navy are more rigid than are perhaps found in other Services. A newcomer such as the short service entrant often found naval life very confusing at first and it was all too easy to put a foot wrong and offend not only those more experienced officers but also the men who served with you. Luckily most of us had recently come from a learning environment and adapted to this new lifestyle with varying amounts of success. Personally, although I found naval life bewildering and even frustrating at times, in retrospect, I enjoyed every minute of it, good and bad.

I have tried not to make this tale too technical; there are plenty of such tales about, but there are many incidents where an explanation is necessary to those unfamiliar with naval flying or indeed naval life. I apologize in advance to those experts who will doubtless accuse me of being too simplistic or flippant. I have often said that those who make their living flying single-engined aircraft over large expanses of deep and usually empty water in all sorts of weather, need to have a keen but slightly warped sense of humour.

I have not dwelt on the sadder times, with friends lost in flying accidents or, being unable to make the required standard, 'chopped' from the flight training. It is largely anecdotal as others far more experienced than me have elaborated on the technology and techniques of flight and flying. I have tried to keep the tale readable and hopefully, in places, amusing.

Times have changed and so has naval aviation. Aircraft are now very much more complex and expensive. The tasking is now different, a widespread global policing in smaller units now taking the place of the large fleets. I was privileged to attend the recent 50th Anniversary of 815 Squadron's involvement with the helicopter. It took place at RNAS Yeovilton, their present base. I was interested to see that there was an abundance of senior ranks, with salaries commensurate with the job they do so well and flying pay reflecting the risks incurred. Our flying pay was only 22 shillings a day, £1.10 in today's currency, and most of us 'foot soldiers' were midshipmen, sub-lieutenants and lieutenants.

I was very impressed with the professional approach of the young men and women that I met there, now doing what I did so many years ago. I wish them all well with every landing a happy one, and as much fun as came my way.

Chapter 1

Every Story has a Beginning

Mine is no different. Most of the young men who sought short service commissions to fly in any of the Services did so with an exuberant desire for adventure and a feeling that flying was possibly the answer. I am sure that it is still the main reason for enlistment.

My reason, I suppose, came to pass when I failed to obtain the required grades to follow a career in medicine. I had never thought of any other career but, with the arrogance and naivety of youth, thought it would, with little effort on my part, all fall into my lap.

Being 18 and at grammar school, I was totally committed to captaining the 1st Fifteen and in love with the girl I would eventually marry. I drifted, neglecting my studies, enjoying undeserved freedoms. Two worthy causes I admit but I paid the penalty at the final examinations.

So there I was, my schooling finished and without the faintest idea of what I was to do with my life. Like most young persons, I craved something different and exciting. I dreaded entering what I considered to be the dull mundane life in an office, clawing my way up the career ladder towards the gold watch and retirement. Now I am very retired and without gold watch, but I still think I was eventually led to make the right choice for me; it was all certainly very different and a world away from my origins and expectations.

In 1935 my parents had settled, like so many, in the new suburban sprawl that had been grafted onto the long established village of Selsdon in the early 1930s. In doing so they had become elevated from the so-called 'working-class' to the most definitely working 'middle-class'. I had been born three years earlier in Clapham and they saw the move as a way to improve their standard of living and enjoy a life outside the mass of London, in what was the edge of the countryside. Our neighbours were mostly in lower or middle management, supplying the staff of London Transport, police, utilities and banking. Most of them had moved to Selsdon for the same reasons as my parents; we were all newcomers to a rural life but only a four-penny bus ride away from a large town, Croydon. My mother's mother and her older maiden sister accompanied us on this migration; they lived next door. I attended the local school and obtained a good but unremarkable education and would have described my life, if it had ever occurred to me, as 'pretty average'. I followed the almost traditional pattern of a middle-class child living in a suburban village; mine was between Croydon and the borders of Surrey and Kent. My uneventful, early years were those of a typical 1930s' boy, regulated by a child's calendar rather than the Gregorian. The seasons revolved around conkers, frogspawn, school holidays and various sports activities dictated by the weather. These activities were paramount, and the growing apprehension of the grown-ups as war clouds gathered over Europe was no concern of mine. Nevertheless, I lived in a time that saw the evolution of the aeroplane and inevitably, was fascinated by the glamour that surrounded flying, and its heroes; inevitably, they were always pilots, both real and fictitious. It was an age when aviation was both fashionable and expanding, mostly in the civil world rather than the military one, as we were never again going to have another war, or so we were told.

Shortly after 1939, when the Second World War was declared, I became, what would later be described as, 'a latch key kid'; an only child with my father now away at war in the Royal Army

Medical Corps, and my mother in full time employment at Kennards, a large department store in Croydon. Like many women, she was new to employment, only having worked very briefly before marriage, but women were now required to fill the positions of the men away at war. She excelled, never having been entirely happy as a housewife, and was soon promoted to the post of buyer for the large department selling household bedding and linens. This took up much of her time, working a six-day week. I was, therefore, from the age of 7, mostly left to my own devices; overseen in a vague sort of way by my grandmother and elderly maiden aunt. They were both very eccentric and they were as much a puzzle to me as I was to them. They were very kind but had absolutely no idea as to what a child, let alone a young boy needed. They could not understand me and I certainly could not understand them.

Being an only child, I did not mix too easily with other children, preferring to use my own imagination and make my own amusements, but nevertheless, I did make many firm friendships, many of which, I am pleased to say, last to this day.

Of course, I found the war very exciting. Fortunately untouched by the widespread and growing tragedy of war, and ignorant of the restrictions of rationing, I spent most of my war in one of the civilian front lines, much later known as 'doodlebug alley'. Selsdon was situated by a few miles in any direction within a triangle of RAF airfields – Croydon, Kenley and Biggin Hill. From the outset of the war, there was always plenty of air activity to stimulate a boy's interest. I could soon identify German aircraft as easily as I could our own. The German aerial offensive had always involved indiscriminate action against the civilian population, as was shown in Spain and Europe, and now in England. They had invented the word 'Blitzkrieg' to describe the process and, as it progressed, the Blitz gave way to V1 and V2 self-propelled bombs, neither of which were intended to be accurate. The V1 bombs usually passed overhead on their way to the capital, the motors automatically stopping as they did so. From then on we, on the ground below, were as vulnerable as the city dwellers, when the bombs glided down. It was a nerve-racking time and even more unpredictable when our fighter aircraft learned to pursue and destroy the bombs before they reached their designated target. This meant that the wreckage fell on the suburbs and on us. The V2 was rocket-propelled and arrived without warning. If you heard it explode, you were a survivor and could set about collecting the shrapnel, a valuable source of currency amongst the kids of doodlebug alley. There was no defence against this onslaught.

After our humiliating defeat in France and the subsequent heroic evacuation of Dunkirk, and before the Blitz months later, I had watched in awe as the Battle of Britain unfolded overhead, filling the skies over southern Britain with man-made clouds of contrails and the darker trails of the unfortunate victims. All too rarely, we saw little white parachutes gently falling. Thanks to the media, the aerial battles were reported within hours and a small boy could listen to the radio and find out the 'score' and hear of how his heroes like 'Paddy' Finucane and 'Cat's-eyes' Cunningham were doing. Thankfully, we never knew how close the battle was; propaganda showed mostly German wreckage lying in the fields and it seemed as though our 'boys' were winning easily.

On Saturdays we could sit agog in the darkness and see it all on Pathé newsreels at the Croydon cinemas after the Wurlitzer organ had descended once more into the depths and Hopalong Cassidy and the Lone Ranger had galloped off the silver screen. We followed the battles with a patriotic fervour, just as kids follow football today.

The initial disastrous first months and the desperate fight back from the brink at Dunkirk were soon over; the summer of whirling dogfights and contrails was ended; the war settled, if that can ever be the word, into what seemed to be for those around the cities, an endless Blitz and distant desert campaigns usually ending in a strategic withdrawal. I read avidly of past and present heroes, enjoying Biggles, Hornblower, Just William and other stories. Before the war, my heroes had been mostly the amateur pilots who were pushing the frontiers of aviation; now it was the fighter and bomber pilots whose exploits demanded my attention.

I dutifully attended primary education and in 1943, aged 11, went on to Purley County Grammar school, chosen before others because my mother liked the maroon coloured blazer.

As the war stumbled on with Japan's attack on Pearl Harbor causing the Americans to come in to join us and provide a much needed back-up and impetus, I continued my education and progressed through my grammar school studying the science syllabus rather than the arts. Nobody, including myself, expected much of me in the final exams. It was thought that my education would cease at 16 and I would leave school to start earning a living out in the cold, cold world. To everyone's surprise, including mine, I matriculated to enter London University after my sixth form studies.

So as the weary 'combined' forces of the Allies pushed through a devastated Europe towards Germany, I persevered in the sixth form with the foggiest intentions of following a career in medicine mainly in order to please my father; my mother, ever shrewd, astute and realistic, could only visualize a career for me that would bring with it a £1,000 a year salary.

Victory in Europe was followed shortly with victory in Asia and the war was officially over. A ravaged UK faced a future more austere than ever, but at least the servicemen were coming home to make what they could of the uncertain times ahead.

My father was still serving in the Royal Army Medical Corps and had been sent overseas to West Africa a year or so earlier, where he happily served with the West African Field Force until just after the end of the war. He was a product of his generation. He had to leave school at 16, his parents being unable to afford his university education, so he had been prevented from studying for his hoped for medical career. His brilliant intelligence and love of things medical had been further frustrated by the need to provide for his family, and he had joined his father in the building trade until my grandfather's death. The business failed in the Depression and he had taken work with Costain, a large construction firm building, amongst other things, the sprawling estate of houses in which we lived. I realize now how thwarted and trapped he felt. He had no sympathy from my mother who appeared to me to be a hard, disgruntled person, incapable of showing affection although she would fight like a lioness in defence of her kin.

When my father was called into the Army, it was a relief for him to be able to change his circumstances; he elected to serve with the Medical Corps where he was able to develop some of his many talents. He passed on his interests to me and was probably deeply disappointed when I squandered my chances of graduating to a medical school in the early 1950s and was left wondering what I could do with my life. I felt that I wanted something different, with adventure and challenge but just did not know what course to follow.

At that time, a regular, prominent advertisement in the national newspapers proudly offered the opportunity of a short service commission to one with my educational qualifications, to fly as aircrew in the Royal Navy for eight years. The Royal Air Force made a similar offer. I think the reason for this continued search for military aircrew stemmed from the fact that Russia, ever suspicious of her one-time capitalist Allies, had become increasingly hostile towards the West. The situation soon developed into what was called the Cold War, and instead of reducing our armed forces, there was an urgent need to maintain a strong military presence. War weary, conscripted men were mostly uninterested in continuing in the forces so there was a pressing need for new young men to fill the ranks. National Service was introduced. Although there were exceptions, all young men over 18 were liable to be called up for military service lasting two years or an alternative spell down the coal mines. In addition there was a special requirement for volunteers to serve longer and obtain specialist skills, such as aircrew. What was then, for me, a most impressive inducement was offered to those who were accepted and completed the contract. On the successful completion of the engagement, there was a promise of a tax-free £1,500 gratuity. The lucky applicant would also be commissioned into the service from the outset.

I never considered that my survival was the premier requirement to getting my hands on this magnificent sum. To those with even a minimum of only five 'O' level GCEs a wonderful, adventurous short-term career beckoned, with every chance of a small fortune and a future in civilian flying to follow. I should perhaps add that, at the time, I would soon, in any case, have been liable for two years' National Service, so my extra six years with a commission instead of just two as a humble 'squaddie' seemed to be a good move.

My parents, very typically, made no comment one way or another and seemed quite content to let me choose my own destiny. My father had by now come back from Africa to be demobbed. He had been recommended, before his return, to apply to the Crown Agents, in London, for a position in the colonial medical service. He promptly did so, was accepted and immediately kitted out to return to his beloved Nigeria as a civilian medical officer.

My parents' marriage had always been a fragile affair, a miss-match of two people with completely different outlooks. They rarely agreed about anything, and I tended to side with my father. My mother had a short temper and a sharp tongue that she used on me almost as much as she did on my father. A separation of several thousand miles avoiding, in those days, the expense and stigma of divorce, suited them both. When my father came home on his periodic leaves, within a week or so they were grating on one another, and it was always with great relief that my father returned to his much loved position in Africa.

At the end of the war, as the men returned to their old jobs, Kennards had retained my mother only on a part-time basis. Mother had, by then, discovered bridge and was now playing several times a week. She could talk of little else and, as is usual in these circumstances, anyone who couldn't, or wouldn't play the game, found her to be devastatingly boring. Apparently bridge is an extremely addictive card game, without any form of cure or rehabilitation on offer.

So, in 1951, I confidently offered my services to both the Royal Air Force and the Royal Navy. The RAF seemed the favourite choice as, living inland as I did, I had much more awareness of RAF operations. The only experience of the sea had been a cross-Channel trip with the school, that had left me feeling distinctly queasy, but not actually seasick, while my contact with naval flying had been practically nil. I had only seen films of carrier operations at the local cinemas and jolly dangerous they looked.

In a very short time I was instructed to attend the RAF interviews at Royal Air Force Station Hornchurch. This presented the first challenge of my budding military career. Just where was Hornchurch and how was I to get to the place in time for the two days of assessment? Out came the ABC of London and I planned my destiny. The Royal Navy remained stonily silent, apparently reluctant to commit itself to what I considered to be a most generous offer of my service.

I arrived at Hornchurch to find myself joining with a small band of a dozen or so applicants. They were all amazingly confident and remarkably well acquainted with one another. It soon dawned on me that they had all been here before. My confidence waned as I realized that I would be at a severe disadvantage against these 'experts'. Some had attended two or three times, and seemed to know all the questions and answers by heart.

The tests over the next two days were obviously meant to explore the mental and physical aptitude of the applicant. After a day of written tests to check on the educational qualifications, there was a medical examination. Practical initiative was assessed by challenging one's ability to get a team of five or six spotty youths across an imaginary chasm using two old tyres, a plank and a piece of rope; presumably the scant remains of one's aircraft. At the final interview, a board of patently weary officers assured me that, whilst I would not be able to pilot, or even to navigate one of their aircraft, I had somehow impressed them greatly with my aptitude for communication and could, in no time at all, become a master sergeant wireless operator. I had no idea what that was or how they arrived at this conclusion as at no time while at Hornchurch, had I even seen a bit of radio or ever expressed an interest in the subject. As an admirer of Biggles, to be a pilot was my only desire. I took my leave and decided to await the outcome of the hopefully imminent Royal Navy interviews. As, disappointed, I travelled home, I thought back on the last two days, and the offer made to me. Had I perhaps reacted too hastily? I decided that I had not – it was pilot or nothing.

I felt that 'wireless operator' sounded a bit lacking in glamour, and 'master sergeant' sounded as if it would take considerably longer to achieve than the interviewers implied. I may have failed their tests, but I was not stupid.

Shortly after this, I was commanded to present myself at HMS *Daedalus*, Lee-on-Solent, in February 1952.

Once again I found myself with another bag of repeat applicants. This time, however, I was, I suppose, well on the way to becoming an old hand myself. Less luxurious by far than RAF Hornchurch, our accommodation consisted of a draughty wooden hut, where we huddled for warmth around a pot-bellied stove, feeding it with fuel whilst awaiting the call to some more tests involving tyres, ropes and bits of wood.

My lasting memory of the whole thing was of the medical examination, in the course of which I was left standing by an open window, trouser-less, in the freezing February weather, while the medical officer, who had been examining me, leant out to discuss at length the just announced demise of His late Majesty, King George VI, with a fellow officer on the path below.

After what seemed an age, he turned around, grabbed my frozen nether regions, and said, 'Cough – right you are. Carry on,' and that was it. The final interviews complete, I returned home to await the call, feeling less than confident. I didn't ever see any of my 'expert' fellow applicants again.

After waiting with growing impatience for a few months for the
results of this interview and, having heard nothing, I presumed to
phone the Admiralty for some sort of answer. Luckily, I got
straight through to the relevant recruiting office - a rare feat
never again to be repeated. The recruiter seemed very confused,
saying he would investigate and get back to me in a day or two.
The next day he contacted me by telephone, to suggest that 'they'
were rather under the impression that I had joined the RAF. I
swiftly disabused him, proclaiming my undying fondness for the
sea, flying and all things naval. The recruiter said that I would be
contacted soon with further details and, in due course, the little
buff envelope arrived stating that I had been accepted for a
commission and training as a pilot and that further instructions
would be sent in due course.

Following on, a week or so later, was another letter telling me
to report to Messrs. Gieves, in London, for the making up of the
uniforms required by a young 'gentleman' commissioned as an
aviation cadet. At last, my mother was very impressed, as was I,
having never been measured for a suit in my life, even at Burtons,
let alone this well-known military tailor. It was an occasion to be
enjoyed by my mother and eccentric aunt who both accompanied
me to London, dressed in their best finery. A month or two later,
I posed, suitably attired, to be much admired by my mother and
the mad aunt who, I now realized, had a 'thing' about uniforms.
I then eagerly awaited my instructions to join the Royal Navy,
certainly the first of my tribe to do so, and now, regrettably, the
last.

The orders at last arrived. I was commanded to proceed to
Waterloo railway station, in uniform, where my entry course
would be met by a petty officer who would escort us, presumably
to wherever we had to go. There was nothing to indicate where
the destination was, or what I would be doing. Obviously orders
were orders and I was expected to carry them out. Apparently the
whys, wherefores and outcomes were now no longer my concern.

On the big day, I boarded the local No. 54 bus at the Selsdon
terminal, clutching a canvas grip issued with the uniform, and a

third class rail warrant, bound for East Croydon railway station and onward to Waterloo. Obviously their Lordships did not consider me to be an officer or a gentleman at the moment. Proudly aware that this was first day of my military career and slightly self-conscious in my brand new uniform, I placed my grip in the luggage space opposite the boarding platform and took a seat alongside so that I could keep an eye on it. Very shortly a little old lady peered in and asked me, 'What time does your bus leave?' mistakenly assuming that I was the bus conductor. Deflated, I sheepishly explained that I was, in fact, a naval officer. She snorted with disgust at my ignorance of the bus company's timetable and tottered off, while I quickly changed my seat to one that was less conspicuous. On arrival at Waterloo, I met up with my future colleagues on the station platform. By the time that we had made the usual diffident introductions to one another, a Petty Officer Guest, who announced himself as our course petty officer, approached us. He informed us, implying that it would be an insult to do otherwise, that we were not to call him 'Sir' but 'Petty Officer' and that we should all board the train about to leave for Weymouth pretty smartish. Once there, we were to take the waiting transport and proceed, without delay, to Portland, where our ship, HMS *Indefatigable*, awaited us; due to sail that very evening for Gibraltar.

As I climbed into the compartment reserved for us young gentlemen I suddenly wondered what, with no opportunity to contact them, my mum and my fiancée would think of my apparent disappearance off the face of the earth. If my mother were playing bridge, she probably would not notice my absence but I certainly hoped my fiancée would. I gazed moodily out of the carriage window as we clattered through Dorset, wondering what the future held.

Chapter 2

Rise and Shine, Young Sirs!

In an evening drizzle, we rumbled across the black waters of the harbour at Portland, huddled on the open deck of the MFV. I later discovered that the initials stood for 'motor fishing vessel'. They certainly never fished but were built to the same pattern. They were, and indeed probably are still, used to ferry sailors, aviation cadets and miscellaneous bodies of inconsequential rank, to and from the moored ships in the harbour. We stumbled up the gangway and dutifully, as previously instructed by Petty Officer Guest, turned to face what we thought was 'aft' and saluted.

I had joined my first ship. As we were led below, the gangways were lifted and with engines thumping, HMS *Indefatigable* made preparations to weigh anchor and stand out to sea. The unseemly haste rather reminded me of the press gang and all I had read of Nelson's day, in Hornblower, Ramage and the other 'seadogs', both fictional and real, who had entertained me in the days that already seemed so long ago.

We were hustled below down perilous ladder-ways into what appeared to be a metal ant heap, along strange passageways that smelt of fresh paint, odd cooking smells and sweat. The walls were a mass of piping and valves; the doorways (now to be known as 'hatchways' or 'watertight hatches') were poised to trip the unwary landlubber. At intervals they all had large levers surrounding their edges, which, Petty Officer Guest informed us,

were to be used to lock the hatches when slammed shut if the
ship was flooded at any time. I fervently hoped that I was on the
right side of the hatch if this ever happened. The passageways
seemed to go on forever to us bewildered newcomers but
eventually led to what was called a gunroom. There were no guns
but several members of what was to be our senior course, three
months ahead of us in the training programme. They lounged
about, observing the new boys. We eyed them warily,
remembering well what senior boys of our recent schooldays
were capable of; the best maxim was that it was best to avoid
them as much as possible. Immediately, we were presented with
a cold meal. I was introduced, unfortunately, not for the last
time, to a cold supper, a meal traditionally served in the evening
on every Sunday in every aircraft carrier I later served in. It
consisted of pilchards in a disgusting sauce of acidulous tomatoes
and, I think, engine oil; equally awful rollmops, a kind of pickled
raw herring, and a limp salad. The dessert I'm happy to say is
unremembered. We were then instructed to go to the 'bedding
flat' to collect our bedding. This turned out to be a storeroom,
miles more passageways and several decks down. A silent,
morose storeman, who obviously considered he was being put
upon, issued each one of us a large sausage shaped, well lashed,
weighty rough canvas lump of an extremely dubious colour,
boasting several previous owners. We were now required to take
part in a well-worn service custom of 'signing' for it. It was our
introduction to our first, and thankfully last, naval hammock.
We returned to the gunroom, where we were handed over to the
seniors for instruction in slinging one's hammock. We were
shown just where we could sling it; they seemed to be an
unhelpful and snooty lot. The seniors, of course, had only just
been promoted to that lofty position on the departure of their
seniors, and as we would do in our turn, had then by right taken
all the now vacant, comfortable quiet berths, leaving only the
various busy passageways around the gunroom, adorned with
large hooks for our use. Having eventually, with great difficulty,
strung up the hammock and managed to climb into the thing, we

were now gift wrapped in rough canvas and folded into a sagging half moon wearily gazing at our feet. These berths meant that throughout the night, we swayed to and fro as people pushed past going about their mysterious duties, while the ship rolled her way down the English Channel. When all was said and done, it had been a long and weird old day. It was some consolation to dream that our turn would come. After a day or two, the hammock became a snug and welcome refuge.

At some unearthly hour we were roused from fitful sleep by the 'shake' and a fearful squeal of the bosun's pipe over the tannoy. It was, without any doubt, a demand that we must lash up and stow our hammocks. I did my best to restore mine to the distorted sausage shape and deposited it, looking like a badly tied parcel, in the chest room flat; a sort of storage room adjacent to the gunroom. Any compartment in the ship that was not labelled a room such as a gunroom was, it seems, called a flat. We then shuffled off to perform the necessary ablutions that were carried out in the starkly basic 'heads'. These toilets and washing facilities were, to anyone with a sense of smell, very noticeably adjacent to our sleeping stations just under the flight deck. The ship's motion was at its most violent at this furthest end of the carrier and it was inadvisable to stay too long there if, like most of us, you were already feeling seasick. Washed, dressed and somewhat reluctant, I staggered down to the gunroom to face an unwanted greasy breakfast. I was by no means alone in my misery.

By this time Her Majesty's Ship *Indefatigable* was rolling and pitching her way down a boisterous Channel and entering Biscay on her way to Gibraltar. Breakfast somehow seemed an unattractive proposition. I felt very unwell. The smells of fried food, fuel oil, body odours and fresh paint did nothing to help. Recurring memories of my distant, school cross-channel trip now vividly reminded me that going to sea had distinct disadvantages. We were brusquely informed that, 'Sea sickness is an offence in the Royal Navy' and punishable, if one referred to our new bible, *Queens Regulations and Admiralty Instructions*, probably with death. We were told 'it was all in the mind'. I thought that there was little to choose between the cause and the punishment and that my mind was the last place involved with how I felt. With the rest of the course, I was hustled around the depths of the ship collecting armfuls of strange articles needed for life aboard our new home.

Number 8 shirts and thick blue trousers work for the use of, brown overalls – work for the use of, boots and shiny gaiters – drill for the use of, and finally the oddest of all, huge bed sheets, (4 of) – but what for the use of? They would easily have covered the largest double bed available. It all seemed endless and mostly unnecessary but, of course, it was duly signed for. Eventually we returned to stow the equipment in the large chests of drawers allocated to us in 'the chest flat'. We changed into our working rig and started to learn of naval life, including a whole new mysterious language. By now I was feeling a little better, and quite looking forward to lunch.

Before classes started we had 'cleaning stations'. The cadets were responsible for keeping clean the area in and around that in which they lived. This included the whole deck around the gunroom. Of course the seniors swept, dusted and generally kept to the cosy confines of the gunroom. They only rarely ventured out into the cold blustery winds that battered us juniors on the outside gun sponsons, where we polished brass and washed the grey paintwork, except to find fault and make our lives difficult. Really not so different from school life, except that I was now a very small fish in a big, heaving and rolling pond. The senior course took it upon themselves to make our lives as unpleasant as possible, covertly aided and abetted by the gunroom sub-lieutenant. It took me several weeks to plot an equally petty revenge. Much later in the course, having endured weeks of the seniors' petty bullying, I purchased some small packets of chewing gum. In those days they came as small sugar coated tablets. I substituted the contents of one packet with some very similar sugared gum of a proprietary brand used as a laxative. Needless to say, a senior soon spotted me, chewing a 'safe' tablet.

He confiscated my doctored packet and that night, as we contentedly swung in our hammocks, the passageway to the heads seemed to be in continuous use by the senior course members pushing by in a hurry. But this lay in the future.

In the dim early morning light of our first day, after our cleaning chores and with my *mal de mer* fading, I discovered *Indefatigable* to be a fleet aircraft carrier that had been transformed into a huge floating school. Together with her sister carrier HMS *Implacable*, the major part of the learning system was aimed at training boys from 17 upwards for service in the Royal Navy. On completion of their time on the two carriers, they would be allocated to the various branches and go on to the shore establishments that would qualify them in a particular trade. For us aviation cadets, this was the introduction to the real Navy for those of us who had not had the benefit of induction through a traditional Royal Navy school or college such as Dartmouth. Also on board was a class of naval ratings from all ranks and trades, known as upperyardmen who, like ourselves, had volunteered for training as aircrew. They followed a similar programme to ours. As they were already very familiar with naval life, their courses were designed to prepare them for the transition to not only a career in aviation but also life as a commissioned officer. They knew that the course for which they had applied and been selected would, on successful completion of their training to 'wings' stage, result in them being commissioned as officers. A very definite incentive, as failure meant reversion to their original rank as ratings, or a voluntary discharge from the service.

As the ship pitched on through the Bay of Biscay towards Gibraltar, we settled into our routine of lectures and training as an introduction to naval life and traditions. None of it was related to aviation, it was purely aimed at producing some sort of naval officer who, at some later date, would fly an aircraft to the deck of a carrier as one of his many functions. One aspect of this training was the roster of 'duty aviation cadet'. In rotation, every cadet had a day when he was attached to the ship's duty officers and attended all aspects of the ship's routine, including watch keeping on the bridge or down in the engine rooms. One memorable night it was my turn to attend the night rounds. This was a nightly inspection of the ship by the captain or his commander although they could designate another senior officer. It was quite a procession as the ship' executive commander, in my case, was always accompanied by a large retinue of departmental officers and senior ratings responsible for the overall cleanliness of the ship. Bringing up the rear and trying to be as inconspicuous as possible, was this night's duty aviation cadet.

We marched through the ship preceded by shrill blasts of the bosun's whistle to alert the unwary that we were coming. Anyone unlucky enough not to dodge the procession respectfully stood to attention as the full majesty of naval discipline passed by. The commander paused occasionally to check a fitting or a corner for dust, dirt or some other dereliction, passing terse comments over his shoulder to the unfortunate ones behind him, as to what action he required forthwith. Eventually, that particular night, we arrived at the ship's galley where the ship's company food was prepared and dished out for collection of the various Messes throughout the ship. It was darkened, as it had closed for the night. The chief petty officer of the rounds stepped in and switched on the light, followed by the commander and his entire retinue crowding in after him. It happened to be the night that the cockroach population had selected for their annual migration. In their thousands they were streaming across the galley deck as a quivering brown blanket, moving from under one bank of tables to another. The commander paused and drew breath before exploding. He ordered the white faced chief to rake out everything that was under the table that was being deserted. The chief did as he was ordered and exposed a pile of long discarded food including a desiccated sausage, long past its sell by date. No one could remember the last time sausages were served. The commander quickly formed the opinion that the conditions under the first table were no longer fit for even a cockroach. There were hurried consultations and the odd harrumph by the commander and then we all marched on. I gathered that the galley staffs were in for a long night. This, I thought, is the chain of command at work.

As part of this introduction to naval life, we were advised of our eligibility to purchase the monthly allowance of 'Tickler'. This was a rough and cheap type of tobacco sold by the half pound tin and available to every member of the crew. It was also possible to purchase other less noxious tobaccos and cigarettes in lieu, which were now available to the cadets in ridiculously large amounts at ludicrously low prices. Soon, we were all sporting a diversity of pipes, cigarette holders and other methods of burning the weed as we aped our various role models of stage and screen. Luckily for most of us, as 'Tickler' had all the qualities and aroma of a burning hayrick together with an even worse aftertaste, the affectation soon died out and the blue fogs cleared from the gunroom before any lasting damage was done to our health. Even now, nearly sixty years later, I still have an old pipe that was last used to pollute that gunroom.

A Mess dinner was also part of our initiation; certainly no boy that I knew of had ever attended such a ceremony or ever expected to. It is a social event and steeped in traditions established by the etiquette of previous centuries. As Lord Nelson is the best known of our naval heroes, many of the procedures are based on his life and times. For instance, as he was handicapped by the loss of his right arm, so the port is passed only with the left hand. Ships of his day had very low deck-heads that made standing upright for the toast difficult and, therefore, in the Royal Navy the toasts are, by Royal consent, made while sitting. I was very impressed by these procedures and their romantic origins. The required dressing up in mess kit was far more traumatic. Firstly one had to get into the shirt, a voluminous thing held together with studs and possessing a starched shield to cross the chest like a sheet of armour. I think the origins for this monstrosity must have come from the thick, riveted sides of the old ironclads. Once inside, a rigid, high pointed collar was attached and around that a hand tied bow tie was a must. Once shirted, all upper body movement was strictly limited, bending at the waist was nearly impossible so that the uniform could only, with difficulty, be climbed into. Footwear had to be highly polished boots without laces, as they were impossible to reach and tie without assistance. After that, with back ramrod straight and gaze fixedly ahead to achieve some small measure of comfort, you could enjoy yourself.

With the ship rolling slightly in the sunny seas off Spain, it was thought that some cadets in the junior course would benefit by completing the trip in style, as true mariners. Unfortunately I was one of the chosen. We were cast adrift with our provisions, a thick cheese sandwich, wrapped in nearly as thick greaseproof paper, and some water, in a ship's 'whaler'; an unwieldy 27-foot open, wooden boat under the command of the young ship's officer in charge of the gunroom, Sub-Lieutenant Paul Perks. As we hoisted the small sail and stumbled about the thwarts, I could not help but think that Captain Bligh must have shared my emotions as my 'home' sailed off over the horizon. We sailed all day, most of us seasick, and all of us definitely sick of the sea. Almost becalmed on an oily swell the sails had to be trimmed continually and the boat baled out, the gyrating motion was endless and the distant coast was apparently stationary. If I had ever entertained romantic notions of getting a little sail boat and sailing off somewhere, that stupid dream was dashed forever in that whaler. Regrettably, after that experience, I never wanted to be a true sailor, but Paul Perks, the young sub-lieutenant, caught the bug to be an aviator. (He was, sadly, killed in a flying accident soon after qualifying for his wings.)

In the late afternoon the whaler and its limp crew washed into the harbour and was hoisted inboard IIMS *Indefatigable*, now alongside a jetty in Gibraltar. It was wonderful to be back on board something that was relatively stable, and I was, at last, able to dash off post cards to my wondering girl friend and my mother, whose last contact with me had been five days ago when I had bid them a fond farewell at the doorway of my home, and vanished into space.

After a few sunny days at Gibraltar, enjoying the unexpected novelty of being in a virtually foreign land; we were ordered to go to 'stores' where we were issued with yet more gear; tropical – hot climes for the use of. We were allowed ashore and enjoyed seeing the sights of the garrison rock. A week later we set off on the return trip, via Lisbon, the beautiful Portuguese capital for just a few days, and thence to Portland where we were to complete our grounding in the art of becoming a naval officer, on board our floating classroom. My impression, so far gained from the regular ship's officers, was that the Fleet Air Arm was a slightly tedious but necessary branch of the modern Navy with a reluctant admission that 'someone had to do it'. I imagine the introduction of cannons and gunners met with the same sort of response. Later, with more experience, I realized that this thinly veiled disdain probably stemmed from the fact that the traditional naval officer had passed through the hardest public school in the country, Dartmouth. He had, by examination, then to climb the promotion ladder, with the fairly remote chance of command of a ship amongst the dwindling numbers remaining. He probably saw us as totally inexperienced, poorly educated newcomers who, after a brief indoctrination, would be promoted, learn to fly and thus earn a far better salary than he had. He, like us, had no conception of the inherent dangers that we would face, flying from a carrier.

On our return to Portland our education continued on board as HMS *Indefatigable* swung at a mooring in the harbour. As we had only been on board for a few weeks, I was surprised when the cadets were allocated a ship's boat and incorporated into the routines of providing ship to shore transport. We had very little knowledge of seamanship and none at all of boat handling. We were given charge of a small, experimental aluminium fast boat. It had been designed to replace a very smart small boat called a skimmer, carried on most ships, which gave a fast waterborne method of transport for senior officers between ships. Our boat was equipped with a water-cooled petrol engine of dubious reliability and was extremely skittish in anything other than flat calm water. Even with its behaviour and the raw crew, the boat was useful for quick runs between other ships and the shore, carrying small groups of officers about their business; if only the engine would complete the trip.

I found the boat, manned by three cadets, great fun but was terrified when having to man it, especially at night. The carrier had booms extended from the boat decks, to which the ship's boats were tethered when not in use. The booms were little more than narrow tree trunks, dressed and highly varnished, that stuck out horizontally from the ship about twenty-five feet or so. A rope ladder dangled down some thirty feet to the oily, filthy water where the secured boats bobbed. At night one was confronted with squatting athwart the boom and inching out over the illuminated pool of water below. If you lost your grip, and every movement indicated that you would, your plunge into the mucky water was very likely to be interrupted by one of the boats below. When at last you reached the ladder, you had to negotiate your body around the boom until a foot engaged the top rung of the ladder, and then transfer your clammy grasp from boom to ladder and descend to catch the mooring line of the boat and pull it to a point where you could board. Some wag on board the ship seemed to think this could all be done in a few minutes from hearing the pipe, 'Away duty boats crew'. Even worse was the thought that you had to repeat the process to get back on board after the trip.

We had been carefully briefed, before manning the boat, on the protocol required when passed by any boat carrying a senior officer. We were instructed to stop the boat and stand facing the other boat at the salute. On my first trip we had the misfortune to be approached by the admiral's barge, distinguished by its colour of dark green, and known to all as the 'green parrot'. As his flag was flying, we prepared to stop and salute. Unfortunately the water cooling pipe to the engine fractured yet again and spewed hot water onto the engine which promptly stopped, emitting dense, hissing clouds of steam. The bemused admiral passed three cadets standing smartly at the salute in a stopped motorboat that was apparently on fire as they were practically obscured, wreathed in smoke-like steam. He must have noted the incident, as he rather doubtfully returned our salute and went on his way; the boat was never used again.

Successful completion of this first phase of our naval training meant that, together with the upperyardmen, we left *Indefatigable* and proceeded to HMS *Siskin*, a shore base near Gosport for more instruction, this time pre flight training. This involved a more intensive study of subjects that would, in due course, allow us to concentrate on the 'hands on' trials of actually flying. The lectures included meteorology, navigation and map reading, telecommunication and Morse code transmissions (shades of the master signaller at Hornchurch once again) and aeronautics. These and other subjects were studied at *Siskin* to provide some knowledge of aviation skills, other than handling an aircraft, needed by an embryo pilot. By learning them here, we saved time at the flying school, having a basic knowledge of the theory.

Chapter 3

A Sailor's Life for Me

On graduating, if that is quite the right word, from our naval training on board HMS *Indefatigable*, our course of would-be naval aviators were duly promoted from cadet to either sub-lieutenants or midshipmen; ranks bestowed upon us by age rather than merit. Due to a hiccup in the system, my course was unable to go immediately to HMS *Siskin*. There was to be a delay of about six to eight weeks before the course could start.

In order to keep us gainfully employed during this intervening period we sub-lieutenants and midshipmen, on leaving HMS *Indefatigable*, were assigned to a small fleet of minesweepers based at HMS *Vernon*, Portsmouth.

HMS *Vernon* was a 'stone frigate' or shore establishment situated adjacent to the harbour entrance to the Solent and next to the jetty of the Portsmouth to Isle of Wight rail ferry. It was a training establishment for young sailors starting their future in the Navy as torpedo or mine disposal specialists and divers. To this end, several elderly minesweepers were employed to sail up and down the Solent giving handling experience in mine destruction techniques to the trainees as part of their course. In fact, the old boats were employed as 'maids of all work' and were normally captained by a single officer, mostly lieutenant-commanders. A couple of Royal Naval Reserve chief or petty officers, together with about twelve ratings, completed the crew. My own appointment was to Her Majesty's motor minesweeper *1044*. I never determined who was more astounded, the crew or myself as the 'Jimmy' or first lieutenant of one of Her Majesty's ships, albeit a small one. It was with some trepidation that I passed through the gates of HMS *Vernon* and made my way down to the waterside to find my ship and introduce myself to the captain.

Her Majesty's review of the fleet was to take place within six weeks. It was thought to be a good idea, and gainful employment, if we were sent to help and gain a little more experience of life in the real Royal Navy. The latter I most certainly did, in abundance. In fact, we supernumeraries, being so inexperienced in ship handling and seamanship, were of little or no use to the worked-up crews of these vessels, but we were accepted with good grace and we helped out as much as we could.

As would be future aircrew, the crew regarded us as if we were rather simple, even mad, mascots. In particular, the chief of the engine room of *1044* had recently served on an active aircraft carrier, HMS *Ocean*. Knowing what I intended to do, he delighted in showing me his large collection of photos of catastrophic aircraft crashes on or over the deck of that carrier. It occurred to me that this was why the advertisements for aircrew had been so abundant and so prominent. Being a Fleet Air Arm pilot, it appeared, might not be as easy, or as much fun, as it had seemed in those advertisements.

During the run up to the review, the motor minesweeper *1044*, together with another similar but slightly smaller boat were designated as 'Tenders to the Review Fleet' now gathering in the Solent for the Queen's review in a few weeks time; with the odd training exercises when things were quiet. It was to be a novel experience, full of incident, that I enjoyed enormously and one that, over the years, has provided me with a fund of after-dinner yarns and, on which I now look back with fond memories.

MMS *1044* was an old, wooden boat of about sixty feet, well past her sell by date. Built to sweep a variety of mines, she was purposely constructed in wood, to avoid unintentionally but catastrophically detonating any magnetic mines close to her hull. They had been the scourge of coastal waters in her war; she was the answer to the menace. She also carried gear to deal with mines using other forms of detonation common in the Second World War. Her best days had long gone, spent, I would think, protecting the approaches to the Thames during the war. On cessation of hostilities she had been laid up on the mud banks at Sheerness, forgotten, to moulder away in peaceful retirement.

Later, resurrected to serve as a training vessel, she had been given a quick lick of grey paint to tart her up and, presumably but not obviously, some sort of service by a dockyard to render her seaworthy again.

A single large screw, driven by an old reciprocating engine salvaged from a long torpedoed coaster, gave her about 8 knots. A high forecastle made any view forward, other than from the front of her bridge, impossible. The poor old girl was unwieldy to manoeuvre in any sort of crosswind, particularly turning to starboard with the wind from that direction. The reason for this was primarily the wind acting on the high bow being compounded by the screws rotation in the water. This always produced a crabbing, sideways slip to any turn to the right. As will be seen, whilst this was hardly noticeable in open water, it could be an acute embarrassment when manoeuvring in confined spaces. The wooden watertight bulkheads that separated compartments had half-inch gaps between the planks, not only denying privacy but also casting a certain nagging doubt about her seaworthiness. Both boats had been given another fresh coat of paint for the forthcoming review but they would never be considered the pride of the fleet. Added to which, there was barely a day when we did not manage to offend our parent ship, HMS *Vernon*. There was little doubt that our very scruffy presence, tied up alongside their immaculate base jetty, was an embarrassment to them and an unsightly blemish on their pristine waterfront, rather like an old, dirty fishing boat tying up in an exclusive marina. Unfortunately, events were to prove them right in their assumption that we were 'bad news' and lowered the tone of the whole place.

My commanding officer was an ageing lieutenant-commander, blessed with the figure, looks and laconic manner of the then very popular film star Rex Harrison. A misguided Admiralty had previously appointed him to the inaptly named HMS *Impregnable*, a training establishment for young female entrants to the Women's Royal Naval Service. Guy, my new CO, with his languid charm, must have caused chaos with the emotions of the impressionable young charges in his care. He obviously had very soon become the despair of the administrators of that establishment. Being a major threat to even the inappropriate name of the base, he was banished as quickly as possible to the command he now held. Even so, exiled as he was, on every weekend that I was on the *1044* there were different, giggling young ladies tripping up the gangway to be entertained by Guy, and what lookers they were. He was a gentleman of superb taste. They never even glanced at the handsome young 'sub'. They were probably well aware of the difference in the rates of pay for a lieutenant-commander and a lowly sub-lieutenant with possibly a limited 'shelf life'.

'Take over Sub, I'm going ashore, – God knows when I'll be back,' was usually my invitation to assume command on a Friday evening. Thankfully weekends were invariably quiet at *Vernon*. I had by now, gathered that we were not exactly welcome in the wardroom of *Vernon*. Living on the boats, we tended to keep very much to ourselves, using only the main gate to go ashore, as our single shared facility.

Shortly before the review, we were ordered to take part with our sister ship in a Royal Marine training operation called Exercise Run Aground. The Royal Marines intended to carry out a seaborne landing on a local beach, using small landing craft. The beach selected for assault was Southsea, a popular holiday resort near Portsmouth. The start time for the formation of the assault fleet was at 0900 outside the harbour as the Marines, in their landing craft, had embarked elsewhere. Unfortunately when we came to depart, the coxswain presented himself to the commander and apologetically admitted that our only signals' rating had failed to report for duty. The rating was a Portsmouth lad and, having recently married, had been given permission to live ashore. With that vital communication link missing, we cast off for our rendezvous. Our task on the exercise was to head for Southsea beach leading two columns of marine landing craft, each led by a minesweeper pretending to sweep the approach to the beach for mines. The overall commander was in the landing craft leading the column behind us, and of a much senior rank to Guy. Our task was to maintain a steady run into the beach, at the last moment, swinging away to port as the landing craft ran on to run aground to land their Marines.

As the beach drew near Guy and I were on the open bridge surveying the shore. It was, even at that early hour, liberally sprinkled with holidaymakers watching the show from the comfort of their deckchairs on the shingle, with all their necessary comforts; Thermos flasks, sandwiches etc. spread around their deck chairs. As we steadily trundled in towards the beach we could easily see that they were in a jolly, holiday mood, looking forward to the morning's entertainment. In the wheelhouse behind us, the coxswain was at the wheel listening for his captain's orders. As he had no view forward, he relied on spoken commands from the captain on the bridge in front of him.

A rating brought our attention to the fact that the officer commanding, in the assault ship astern, was frantically signalling by lamp. Now would have been the time for the absent signals' rating to step forward.

'How's your Morse, Sub?', asked Guy.

'So-so', I honestly replied, 'If you can write down the letters, I'll call them out.'

At last, after a fashion, I was to be useful. My aptitude for the Morse code, however, left much to be desired and was miles away from that of the master signaller that the RAF had so confidently predicted not all that long ago.

The first mistake that I think my CO made, was to join me, looking astern, as I hesitantly called out the letters. By leaving his station on the bridge, he left the coxswain grasping the wheel inside the wheelhouse and resolutely steering the last course and speed given to him, but unable to see where he was going because of the high forecastle.

Slowly I called out the irate signal 'F-o-r G-o-d-s S-a k-e H-u-r-r-y -Up' which was being flashed by the lamp astern. Guy grunted with annoyance and we both turned to look ahead and carry out the command but there was now no time to try and speed up. It was far too late. The *1044* was about to carry out Operation Runaground to the letter and run aground. The bow slid out of the waves, crunching its way up the shingle beach with startled holidaymakers scrambling in all directions up the shingle, to avoid the looming bow. They were clutching an assortment of deckchairs, dogs and children. Newspapers, blankets and assorted picnic gear were scattered in awful abandon. Guy and I could only look on in speechless horror.

The awful grinding of the keel finally stopped as we ground, inevitably, to a halt and gently tilted to one side. The landing craft swept past, doors opening, with Marines leaping out onto the shingle, laughing helplessly at our plight. Our sister ship passed astern, politely hailing us to say that they would walk out later to take tea. We glumly watched them turn into the harbour mouth and disappear.

We were pulled off by tug much later that afternoon at high tide, having provided a marvellous photo opportunity to the now returning holidaymakers. Humiliated but undamaged we sheepishly sailed back to *Vernon* to face their wrath. They immediately put a padlock on our tiny bar in the wardroom, inferring, quite wrongly, that we had been drinking. I'm sure there was a certain vindictive glee in their reaction.

A few days later, returning from a routine minesweeping session with the class of young seamen grouped on the stern, we started a turn in to Portsmouth harbour to come up alongside our sister ship, now berthed at *Vernon*. There was a strong wind and tide coming in through the harbour mouth that counteracted the swinging bow because of the high forecastle. Aided by the screw pushing the boat's stern in the same direction, our vain attempts to turn were cancelled out by wind and tide. With the *1044* now not answering her helm, we struck our sister ship amidships causing a largish hole just under her bridge. My opposite number, watching open mouthed and transfixed on the wing of the bridge, was more than a little startled as he stared at the dim, interior of his ship, through the hole between his feet.

'Bloody Hell, full astern!' shouted Guy.

'Aye, aye, Sir. Full astern it is, Sir!' replied the coxswain, unaware of the havoc we had caused. Bells rang in the wheelhouse, the water under our stern churned. Shuddering, the *1044* leapt backwards out of the splintered hole.

Alas, our day was not done. The Isle of Wight ferry was coming in dashingly fast, like a destroyer, intending to smartly go full astern at the jetty and stop to land the passengers. In our haste, we shot backwards into her path. With a crash of splintering wood, she carved about ten feet off our stern, luckily above the waterline and without casualties and, hopefully, what we could call 'cosmetic' damage. We limped into our berth and tied up to await the wrath of *Vernon* as yet again, they descended upon us. Those dreaded words, 'board of enquiry' and 'courts martial' were bandied about with a certain relish and the bar remained firmly closed.

Guy remained remarkably sanguine about the whole affair. I think he had heard those words before, probably at HMS *Impregnable*. Being only a lowly sub-lieutenant and, as an aspiring aviator, totally unreliable at that, I was never even to be called for evidence, let alone prosecuted.

Boards of enquiry though, would have to wait as the review was almost on us and our role was considered vital. We were banished up the creek to moor alongside in the dockyard for urgent repairs by the 'chippies'; a stark contrast to the elegant, but faded, Royal Yacht once used by Queen Victoria tied up close by. In disgrace, we were covered with dockyard 'mateys' sawing wood, hammering and painting for several days. My other colleague, and would-be flyer, and I took advantage of HMS *Vernon's* shallow water diving course while both boats were under repair. In cumbersome suits we happily worked in the tank at *Vernon* and stumbled about the murky shallows of Portsmouth harbour for a week.

The boats being made of wood, repairs were fairly simply carried out and we were soon fit for our duties as tenders to the fleet, but *1044* was commanded to remain at our dockyard moorings, out of the vengeful *Vernon*'s sight, and obviously still in disgrace. We were, however, allowed to re-open our small bar in the wardroom.

The duties were still not without almost daily incident. The most embarrassing moment left for me, in my diminishing career as a sea officer came later, as we awaited our last batch of VIP passengers to embark at *Vernon* and be transported out to join the big ships anchored in the Lines. Our task was to get them out to their host ships well before Her Majesty sailed later in the morning to review the massed fleet. Needless to say, being very important, they were very late coming aboard, as VIPs always are. The poor old *1044* was so slow, and we were dangerously late when we arrived at the first warship. Luckily, the deliveries were to the Royal Navy vessels leading the first line at Spithead. After calling at the last ship the plan was that we should sneak through the lines and scurry back into harbour unseen by Her Majesty, to hide our scruffy selves before the Queen entered the first line of ships in *Britannia*. Because of the delays, we were still plodding down the first line trying to make our escape when *Britannia* surged serenely through the harbour mouth. At one awful stage it seemed as though *1044* would carry out the Royal review by herself, with the Queen in fast pursuit down the first line. We were ordered to get out of the area immediately and anchor in the first discreet and most insignificant spot we could find. However, *1044* could not do 'immediately' and none of the attendant, smartly dressed, lesser naval craft would allow us anywhere near, in fear that they would be contaminated by association with us. Finally, we imposed ourselves on the hapless but silent crowd of the loyal, private sailing craft anchored off Fawley as sightseers. We still felt very conspicuous but were, at least, stationary and hopefully invisible, although our tatty grey shape did stand out amongst our smartly painted companions. Of course, we were not gaily covered in bunting, or manned by extra men, dressed in their best uniforms ready to cheer as the Royal ship passed. The few men of our crew were dressed only in their working rig and the boat was definitely not review material. But we were painted grey, flying a White Ensign and Guy felt, quite rightly, that we ought to show willing as a Royal Navy unit. Our disgruntled, muttering ratings were sent below to change into their best rig, usually only worn ceremonially or on runs ashore. Just as the Royal Yacht passed the last of the assembled fleet and started for home, we must have been the last boat to salute her. I do not suppose she ever knew that we were there, or that our, by now, nearly mutinous crew had to man one side and cheer, waving their caps in joy, and then rush to the other and repeat the cheer in order to make out we were fully manned. You could tell that our sailors were, like Her Majesty's great-grandmother, not amused. There was a definite atmosphere; the late Captain Bligh RN would have recognized the signs, as the crew went below to change back into working rig.

We made our weary way back to our backwater berth hopeful that *Vernon* would never hear of our latest debacle. Then came the Royal signal 'splice the main brace' and the rebellious crew, as the rum was issued, promptly forgave everything the two of us had put them through.

The 'splice' on *1044* was not without incident. Guy had left me in charge of the boat with a brief, 'I'm off Sub, I'll be back later this evening', and vanished over the side to disappear into the silent dockyard. I had invited my fiancée to join me in the tiny wardroom and we were sitting planning our weekend. There was a knock on the door and the coxswain presented himself, beaming happily, waving a signal and carrying a very large stone bottle by its lug.

'Signal, Sir, from 'er Majesty, God bless 'er, Sir, to splice the main brace, Sir. Permission to carry on, Sir?'

'Yes, please carry on, Coxswain', I replied.

He promptly produced three glass tumblers and proceeded to nearly fill each one with neat rum from the large stone bottle.

With a muttered 'Ma'am – Sir', he thrust a glass of neat rum into our hands, raised his own glass and said 'God save the Queen, Sir, an' God bless 'er'. He quaffed his generous tot in one go whilst, bemused, we followed suit. 'I'll jus' go below, Sir, an' see t'the Lads, Sir'.

He departed, almost certainly to join 'the lads' in another celebration, an expensive round for Her Majesty. I placed my glass on the table and turned, amused by the event, towards my beloved. She was in a rum induced coma, slumped on the wardroom couch, her empty glass still in her hand and impossible to wake. She took no further part in the proceedings. Guy returned later that evening and I took my still sleepy fiancée back to the hotel.

I never did hear what the outcome from any enquiry into our colourful command might have been as, regrettably, I did not keep in contact with Guy. For me, my exciting life as second in command of a minesweeper was over. Pre-flight training at HMS *Siskin* at Gosport was in the immediate future and flying training school beckoned at somewhere called RAF Syerston, in the mysterious Midlands.

Chapter 4

'I Have Control'

Pre-flight training at HMS *Siskin* was the start of the ladder towards an aviation career with the Royal Navy. We lived in the wardroom at *Siskin*, an old, sleepy, grass airfield whose sole connections with aviation at this date were the pre-flight training courses and the use of the airfield as a satellite to helicopters operating out of the nearby Lee-on-Solent airfield. Our classrooms were in the old nineteenth century fortifications known as Martello towers, built to defend the area against invasion by the French in Napoleonic times. There, we studied the ground subjects that were needed before actually piloting an aircraft. Amongst those early classes were navigation, meteorology and the principles of flight, including aerodynamics and rules of the air. Our ground studies would not cease after *Siskin*. Our whole flying programme until 'wings' would mean that half our time at Syerston would be in the classroom compared with all our time here at *Siskin*, with examinations at several stages to ensure that any aspiring candidates who were below par were weeded out before the flying in earnest began. We were warned that the failure rate would increase dramatically once we commenced flying and that what we did at *Siskin* would ease the workload at the next phase and allow us to concentrate on handling aircraft. At last, definite targets were ahead of us. We pressed on towards the autumn in that delightful rural retreat called *Siskin*. Success here meant that we then loaded our old bangers or other forms of transport with our kit and made our way, up the Fosse Way, created by the Romans, north into the Midlands

The now yellowing pages of my flying logbook show that, by the end of September 1953, I had arrived at RAF Station Syerston, near Newark in Nottinghamshire. The RAF was responsible for the primary and advanced flying training up to the award of 'wings', of most naval pilots in the United Kingdom; although some trained up to their 'wings' qualification at Pensacola in the USA. At the time, I would dearly have loved to have gone to Pensacola, but later on realized that those pilots who had done so were at a distinct disadvantage when they returned to the UK to familiarize on operational fighter aircraft. Learning to fly in the clear blue skies of Florida was a poor introduction to flying in the changeable and usually poor flying conditions produced by weather in the UK. This lack of experience led to many a sticky and often fatal end for the returned pilots; their limited skills were no less than ours but they were converting to high speed aircraft where the slightest lapse could be at least very frightening, at worst positively lethal. Having lost many friends on their return to England, I was then very thankful for my initial training in the murky Midlands. In those distant days, coal was still king, and the heavily industrialized areas of middle England were still covered with coal mines and open cast excavation with the factories and steelworks, relying on the coal, in full production, belching out smoke and steam day and night. Whilst it was not perpetual fog, it was a far cry from the usually clearer weather in the south. It required careful navigation and well developed aviation disciplines to avoid embarrassing incidents. It was not unknown for aircraft to approach and even land at the wrong airfield. After a long cross-country flight, especially at night, a pilot, anxious to get back on the ground could easily make the criteria fit what he wanted to see. One of my fellow students on such a flight, luckily with his instructor, approached an airfield and decided it was Syerston. He told the instructor that the base was ahead, the instructor, trying to give him a hint, asked him how he knew. The student confidently listed several identifying features that proved, to him, that it was the home base. The instructor gently pointed out the identifying beacon, clearly flashing with a bright red light a Morse identifying code that was obviously not Syerston's. The convinced pilot said without hesitation that the beacon must have a fault. It was a busy bomber base on night flying operations and a student pilot in the circuit would have been most unwelcome.

I joined 'A' Flight No. 1 squadron for the three months' ab initio course, and mustered at the crew room on 1 October 1953 with the rest of my course, in my flying overalls, together with my bulky parachute, leather flying helmet and fur lined, knee length boots, stuffed into a huge canvas bag with a host of other equipment deemed necessary for even an embryonic pilot. By now, I had accumulated so much gear that I needed, but did not own, a large van to carry it around. At home I now had stacks of kit piled up that I would not need for some years, if at all. Tropical clothing is certainly an unwanted luxury in Nottinghamshire and the more northerly latitudes I was likely to be living in for the foreseeable future. I now felt very akin to Biggles or even a Kamikaze pilot. I was not alone, the cameras were out and students were posing all over the aircraft on the line.

A slightly built commissioned officer called out my name and that of another student. Tony Lister was to be our instructor for this phase of our training.

Commissioned pilot Lister was a quiet, serious and somewhat dour man who seldom smiled. Probably teaching new pilots to come back alive and bring him back also, makes an instructor like that. Our trusty steed was to be the Percival Prentice. He shepherded us out to a Prentice and spent some time showing us the various external parts of an aircraft that have to be routinely checked before starting up. They are all capable of causing acute embarrassment when flying. They have to be waggled, pushed, pulled and inspected carefully before every flight. Unchecked, they have all caused disaster in the past and the checks are the result, gained from a wealth of painful experience.

Early in any pilot's career they are taught to take nothing for granted and to personally check everything. The two maxims were, 'If God had wanted us to fly, He would have given us wings', and Murphy's Law that 'If anything can go wrong, it will go wrong'.

Eventually, Mr Lister and I at last climbed up the wing and clambered into the cockpit ready for my introductory flight. Firmly belted into the seat, alongside Lister, I sat, excited but bewildered, gazing at what seemed an impossible array of instruments. I little realized then, that compared with any subsequent aircraft I flew, they represented only a basic instrument panel. Ahead was nothing but a long nose and propeller. The instructor quietly, but firmly insisted that I was to keep my hands and feet well away from the controls unless he told me otherwise. He then went on to explain the instrument panel, stressing that I would be required to know it, with the aid of the little blue covered *Pilot's Notes* by tomorrow. These books come with nearly every aircraft in the Services. They are the recognized manual for operating a particular aircraft and are a continual source of reference. Now came the ritual of starting the engine. After fifty odd years, I cannot remember precisely the starting procedure for that engine. There were two methods; by hand-swung propeller, or by using a mobile collection of batteries called a 'trolleyac' to power the aircraft's electric starter motor.

The first method was dangerous for the airman swinging the propeller and I remember that soon after we arrived there was an unfortunate incident where the engine misfired and the aircraftsman lost an arm. I think that after that incident, the 'hand swinging' starting method was only demonstrated. The trolleyac was commonly used, supplying external electrical power and unplugged once the engine was running. When Mr Lister was satisfied that all was well with the start up, he explained the instrument readings in the cockpit, leading me through the controls and finally waving 'chocks away' and we were moving. There was some garbled talk over the R/T at that stage; it meant nothing to me but it was, in fact, Lister obtaining clearances from air traffic control. Entering the runway we lined up for take-off, and, with a further warning not to touch anything, we trundled down the runway. The aircraft climbed, in a slow turn, away from the airfield, with Mr Lister patiently explaining all the while, what he was doing and why; it all fell on largely deaf ears. It was all totally confusing. He said that the airfield was down there on my side of the aircraft but, try as I might, I could not see anything other than a hazy patchwork of fields and trees, but after a while I did make out hangars and runways and I began to grasp something of what he was saying. At what he considered a safe height, well away from the airfield, he levelled out and allowed me to gently try the controls and throttle; I was actually flying at last. He completed a loop, a slow roll and a stall. The stall was the most important demonstration at the moment as it gave the novice a chance to feel the aircraft's responses to a dangerous loss of airspeed and, therefore, control. This loss had to be avoided at all costs on approach and landing. When committed to a landing it was completed at speeds just above the stall and it was all too easy for a pilot to overlook his speed when concentrating on the correct approach to land. There was nothing else in the Prentice repertoire and Mr Lister asked if there was any thing else I would like him to show me. Out of my very limited aviator's vocabulary I had to quickly find a word that might impress my instructor. I remembered my Biggles and suggested a spin. He quickly glanced at me and I could see that he now thought that he 'had a right one here'. However, he obliged me, and with a suitably impressed student we landed after thirty-five minutes.

The students, upperyardmen and officers, were mixed and split into two classes. While one section flew, the other attended ground school, extending the subjects started at *Siskin*.

When flying, two students shared an Instructor who taught each individual the intricacies of flying. Each day we flew, learning our trade and gaining in confidence. The Prentice was an aircraft with very few vices to trap the unwary, but the spin needed to be handled with great care. Having entered a spin, we were warned that after a few turns, the plane tended to flatten out so that it was horizontal; turning about its centre of gravity. In this condition it was extremely difficult to recover as, in this configuration, the ailerons and rudder became ineffective and recovery was often impossible. We were warned that whilst we had to practise spinning in order to recover from it, we were never to allow the spin to develop and had to commence the action at great height with recovery procedures within two rotations. I now understood why, on that first flight, my instructor had looked at me in such a startled fashion. Apart from that I soon learned that the Prentice did everything at 70 knots and that practically all manoeuvres, except take-off, landing and cruising, required height and a fairly steep dive to get the necessary speed, before attempting them.

After seven hours of dual, Tony Lister pulled off the runway, muttering that he was not going to be thrown around like this anymore and I was to go off by myself and complete one 'touch and go' followed by a landing that was good enough for me to taxi over and pick him up. Stunned I was suddenly on my own; my first solo. No pilot ever forgets, or is quite ready for, that moment. I taxied to the take-off point, obtained permission to enter and rolled down the runway; 70 knots ease back – easy – the Prentice obediently climbed away. Then came the awful dawning thought that I, and only I, was now able to get me down safely in one piece. Forever, after that occasion, when people asked if I felt responsible for the safety of others in my aircraft, I always replied that my main concern was to get me back safely, the rest would follow as a matter of course. My first solo flight thankfully went to plan and a relieved Mr Lister and I taxied back to dispersal, before I taxied off again, by myself, for my first session of solo 'circuits and bumps'. I don't ever remember thanking him for his efforts on my behalf but if the old chap – he must now be well into his eighties. – ever reads these words, I thank him for starting me off on the right track.

The routine soon began to take shape, with advanced ground subjects and flying, alternating each day. Nearly all students had flown solo but some struggled and after a check by the senior instructor, a few failed to make the grade and quietly departed. At first, special friends were sorely missed but in no time we accepted the departures, as we realized that to continue with a pilot who was unable to cope at this level, could only lead to eventual disaster further into the course. We were also far too busy keeping up on the demands for our own survival. I realize now that the Prentice was an extremely sedate learning platform and almost without vice. Our initiation to flying was a gentle one, designed to create confidence rather than ability. The Prentice successors were to be altogether more agile and speedy. This made the gap between the primary and advanced trainer far closer. This, I think, was far better for the pupil pilot as it was not such a startling transition as that between Prentice and Harvard. Naturally, I write from personal experience, but friends who qualified on later courses, maintain that their transition from the piston Provost to Vampire jet was far more frightening.

After a welcome leave at Christmas, the course transferred to D Flight, No. 2 Squadron, to familiarize on the famous Harvard. This course of advanced flying was to take six months. By now the Prentice was 'old hat' and the North American Harvard looked and behaved as I imagined a real aircraft should. In appearance it was similar to the American naval aircraft of the Second World War. It had an enviable reputation for ruggedness and reliability. For us embryonic pilots, its engine and looks encouraged us to think, albeit erroneously, that we were real pilots at last.

This was an altogether different beast to the sedate Prentice, with a reputation for an unpredictable and vicious spin if the pilot allowed the airspeed to drop too low. Also, it was fitted with a retractable undercarriage to think of with all the other checks.

A much more powerful radial engine meant a boot-full of rudder was required to counter an alarming tendency to swing off the runway one way on take-off, and the other way on landing. Depending on the speed, the Harvard would swing viciously into what was termed a 'ground loop', careering off the runway often on one main wheel, wing tip scraping the ground, to the scornful cheers of unsympathetic onlookers. The solution was to expect it, especially in a crosswind, and quickly counter the swing with rudder. The spin could also be unpredictable. I should perhaps explain about the not so gentle art of spinning. A spin is induced in an aircraft when airspeed is reduced below that necessary to maintain normal level flight, other than on landing, which of course is carried out at a speed just above the stall and is completed by virtually stalling inches from the surface on landing. Some aircraft fail to spin and descend rapidly in some other configuration; many others enter the spin by a sudden drop of a wing and the aircraft commencing a whirling, fast descent, nose down and out of control until the pilot takes corrective action. Most aircraft could drop 1,000 or more feet before effective recovery can be made. At height, this presents few problems but as nearly every landing involves an approach at very slow speeds, close to the ground, a spin at this point could be, and nearly always was, lethal. Hence it is vital for a pilot to be very aware of his airspeed on approach, and of the few small indications that warn of a potential spin. It had been fairly difficult to induce a spin in the Prentice but the Harvard was an altogether different bird, and recovery from spinning was a much-practised exercise.

After a few hours dual with Flight Lieutenant Murray Warson, my new instructor, I soloed and started to find out what a joy it was to fly this machine for myself. It was exhilarating to take-off, climb away, and wheel and turn in the clouds of a summer sky, seeing the green fields and villages slip by below as you returned to base. Even now, in old age, I gaze skywards and envy those who are probably quite unaware of the privilege it is to enjoy flight at the controls of aircraft. It far outweighs the times of struggling through filthy weather to find and land, thankfully, at a rain soaked destination, your flying suit clammy with concentration.

It was my introduction to what I found to be the norm in my aviation career. The aircraft that scared you to death for the first few hours were the ones you would love forever. I suppose cavalrymen felt the same about their mounts.

The Harvard introduced us to a far more expansive type of flying. Its power meant it was extremely versatile and, because of this, there were many more students whose capabilities failed to meet the required levels of competence. Now it seemed that colleagues were dropping away every week or so; some very disappointed; many relieved to opt out of the struggle. There was an intensity building up and a realization that this was all for a purpose, and risky with it. We became familiar with many aspects of formation flying – a tricky skill for us novices, flying only on instruments in order to operate in bad weather – without reference to the ground and aerobatics, often in formation, to hone the coordination skills required in our chosen field. Then there was night flying, very relaxing because there were not so many sharing the sky, but sometimes a confusing practice with only lights and radio communication to guide you. Then marvellous, greasy bacon and egg sandwiches to greet you on a late return from a night navigational exercise, the famous 'night flying supper'.

As this phase of training came towards its end, our happy but now much smaller band suffered its first fatalities. One of the upperyardmen, with many hours of piloting before joining the Navy, was seen to come vertically out of some cloud at about 3,000 feet with the Harvard still at full power. He plunged into the ground, exploding on impact. The weather was perfect with only a few scattered white clouds and it remains a complete mystery how such an accident could happen, and to such an experienced pilot. A bunch of very subdued student pilots were in a reflective mood that evening. Then a week or two before our passing out parade, with our flying course virtually completed, another upperyardman managed to beg a ride with an instructor on another squadron. The instructor was familiarizing on the replacement training aircraft, the Percival Provost, destined to succeed the Harvard. The brand new piston engined Provost was due to be flown by the courses following us. Flying well below the permitted height for low flying, they crashed into a wood and both were killed. I would hasten to add that these accidents in no way reflected on the abilities of the upperyardmen. In fact at the passing out parade, the now ex-ratings took most of the honours and, in many cases, went on to be some of the best pilots in the Fleet Air Arm.

A military funeral was a very sad prelude to the course 'wings parade' at the end of June 1954. I think that twenty-two out of the original thirty-two students completed the course at RAF Syerston. It was a proud moment for us all to step forward for the coveted 'wings' to be pinned onto our left sleeve, and especially for me, as my mother had forsaken a day's bridge to bring my fiancée up to the ceremony. I packed my kit and headed south to await my joining instructions for RNAS Lossiemouth. With brand new shiny wings sewn onto my left sleeve, I was getting ever closer to my boyhood heroes.

Chapter 5

Onwards and Upwards

In 1954 all Royal Navy pilots completing initial flying training were posted to Royal Naval Air Station Lossiemouth in Scotland for further training on Vampire jets and the later conversion onto the current Fleet Air Arm operational fighter, the Seahawk. RNVR pilots were sent to RNAS Eglinton, in Northern Ireland, for training in the anti-submarine role, flying Fairey Firefly aircraft that were, very shortly, to be phased out and replaced by the new Fairey Gannet.

I was, therefore, appointed to Lossiemouth for fighter training. After a short break at Selsdon, I once again made my way to the railway station, this time for the trip to the far north to the Moray Firth.

Personally, I had my doubts that I was suited for the fighter pilot role. Whilst I had thoroughly enjoyed my time at Syerston, I had come to realize that the fighters work was largely carried out at ever increasing altitudes. I suspected that I would not be happy in that role; I felt that high altitude flying would entail hanging in limbo; an empty void with no contact with the planet except by radio. I voiced these doubts to various authorities but was met with astonished disbelief that anyone could not want to fly fighters, or an abrupt, 'You'll go where you're bloody well sent', and off to the Scottish Highlands I went. Perhaps I was wrong in my gut feeling. I might even enjoy being a 'fighterjock'.

When finally disgorged by the train and bussed to RNAS Lossiemouth, I found the airfield to be a fairly large establishment, sprawling at the edge of the beautiful Moray Firth. The air was fresh and crisp with what seemed to be unlimited visibility to the mountains in the distance. Yes, I thought I might like it up here. For a start it had a far better weather factor than Syerston although, already I had heard dark mutterings about some treacherous fog called Har that could sweep in within minutes. With the joining procedure completed, the course from Syerston gathered in the crew room of No. 759 Squadron, for the start of our conversion to the world of jet aircraft. The commanding officer welcomed us and introduced us to his staff, whose role it was to convert us into jet pilots. The silver Vampires waited patiently outside on the hard standing, looking very sleek and low in the summer sunshine. In a very short time we were allocated to instructors, issued with, and studied, the pilots' notes on the Vampire and the limited flight duration of the Vampire T 22.

After some additional instruction on the ejection seat to which we all paid particular attention and the alarming practical experience of being fired in a seat up a vertical rig; I climbed into the aircraft for the first dual sortie on 22 July 1954. Like all jets, they gobbled fuel and flights were of much shorter duration;, it was a feature that had to be carefully watched. My instructor was Lieutenant Doug Baker and, as is often the case with instructors, he was a quiet and courteous man with infinite patience.

I found my first jet aircraft to be quite different from the piston types I had flown to date. From the start up, when the engine began with a low whine and built up to a deafening scream, to the ultimate sensation at height, that you were silently floating, hanging, almost disembodied, the engine note now just a dull whine. The landing, too, was very different. There was a splendid view ahead, without the obstruction of a long engine nacelle and the whirling disc of the propeller; a nose wheel meant that this view was what you had for an approach and landing. If a usual circuit preceded the landing, the Vampire was brought in on the 'dead' side of the runway as normal and speed had to be whittled off with the use of airbrakes so that wheels and flaps could be selected on the downwind leg and on to the final approach. Often you flew the aircraft in a continual descent, onto the runway, usually using air traffic control until the runway was in sight and all checks had been made for landing. There was no careful judgement of speed and height required for the flare of a 'three point landing' as for an aircraft with a tail wheel. The throttles were set for the approach and a continual descent was aimed at until, at the right speed, you contacted the ground. It was a far smoother ride than previous aircraft. As stated earlier, in the early jets, fuel consumption was a main concern. The needles in the fuel gauges seemed to unwind as you looked at them and flights were conducted always with one eye on the fuel remaining for a safe return. Whilst this vigilance is advisable in all aircraft, there was a far greater tolerance with a piston engine. At first I was enthralled with this new world; everything happened at a far speedier pace than the Harvard and hanging high in the sky on a clear day you could see a large part of Scotland with its blue-grey granite mountains, their slopes turning through autumnal colours until the green valleys and tumbling streams were reached. Our lives were now concentrated on fighter drills, close formation and combat formations of four aircraft. We carried out two or so missions a day and were soon into aerial gunnery. I was hopeless at aerial combat. With everything on a far larger canvas at those great heights, I found it difficult to find my 'enemy', a small silver splinter in the vast sky. When I did find him and made a few passes, firing the guns at the white banner he valiantly towed, the results were disappointing to say the least. The unmarked banners didn't need laundering let alone repairing. The painted bullets that I had fired had fallen without trace, uselessly into the sea far below us. I was not alone in finding aerial combat difficult, but to return from one mission after another with nothing to show on the banner or flickering gun-camera was disappointing.

As the course progressed, I soon found that after take-off one climbed through cloud to a high altitude where an air direction controller on the ground guided you to imaginary interceptions of 'enemy' aircraft for an hour or so, or you whirled around the heavens in formation, your eyes glued on your leader. You were then guided back to the airfield and descended blind through cloud. Because of the Vampire T22's tendency to get the windscreen badly iced up, there was hardly any forward vision through the windscreen. During the flight the frost gradually crept down the front windscreen until you were peering through the one-inch gap that was left after the battle between the heater and the sub-zero air outside. You were controlled by air traffic control radar until you finally, with good fortune, broke through the final cloud layer at a low height, looked ahead through the now de-icing windscreen and saw the runway lights ahead. I could envisage a future aerial combat that would be against some distant, unseen opponent and even the actual use of the weapons would be at the whim of someone on the ground. It just didn't appeal to me. Biggles and his chums would have been unimpressed too.

Now with more knowledge of the types of flying available, my interests were in the rapidly developing helicopter roles, and in the sphere of anti-submarine warfare.

During summer leave in August, having formally asked permission of the captain at Lossiemouth, I married my fiancée at the delightful old Norman church at Addington. My best man was Lieutenant Harvey Hadnutt, an old friend from the day we had joined, and first met on a platform at Waterloo station. He was due to get married six weeks after me so we had a reciprocal arrangement for me to be his best man.

After a short honeymoon, I returned to Lossiemouth still unconvinced that I was fighter material, but kept quiet about it in case my peers thought I was chickening out.

A few weeks later I was saddened to hear that Harvey, who was now at Stretton, a base near Manchester, had been killed when his Seahawk went out of control. I later heard that the engine had caught fire, burning though his control system. Harvey stayed with the aircraft trying to get it clear of the heavily built-up areas below. He succeeded and ejected, as the aircraft crashed into fields below, but he was, by then, too low for the parachute to deploy. My wife did her best to comfort his distraught fiancée.

In view of my unspoken wish to transfer to the anti-submarine aviation world, luckily or, depending on one's view, unluckily, my own lack of skill at gunnery came to my rescue. Eventually, at that time, every fighter pilot was expected to come face to face with an enemy pilot, almost inevitably, at some unbelievable altitude, having been directed onto his target. By skilled flying and the use of fixed cannon or machine guns, the dispute was resolved. As mentioned earlier, to my chagrin, later seen as good fortune, I had great difficulty in hitting the target drogue towed by another Vampire. Day after day, I returned to base leaving the drogue in pristine condition, untouched by my bullets with their coloured tips. Back at base, in the crew room, the gun sight camera jerkily revealed that Biggles and I had very little in common in the gunnery world. Naturally, I was disappointed to have to admit a flaw in my ability and, of course, I knew that my future as a military fighter pilot was in jeopardy, but many of the students failing at this stage were being re-appointed to the alternative training establishments as the demand for aircrew in those branches increased with the demand for anti-submarine and helicopter crews

Inevitably I was now recognized as unsuitable for the fighter pilot role and summoned to discuss my future with the commanding officer. I hoped to convince him that I would succeed in another branch of flying. Worryingly just before my interview, my last sortie of air gunnery showed that seven of my shots had hit the target. Was this sheer good luck or was I at last getting the hang of it? This was an almost unheard of score for a student.

With this in mind, I presented myself for my interview, feeling a trifle concerned that fate was playing silly games with me. However the captain soon assured me that my startling score would have no bearing on his decision and asked if I had any preferences about my future. I quickly emphasized what I had always thought was a more suitable role for me. He noted it down and, like so many others, I was suspended and left Lossiemouth, depressed that I had failed to reach a required standard, but relieved that I was to be considered for an alternative flying role. Ordered to await further instructions I proceeded on leave until their Lordships' decision was known.

I spent the Christmas leave happily at home with my new wife, awaiting their verdict. In mid-December 1955, I was delighted to be appointed to No. 737 Squadron based at RNAS Eglinton (HMS *Gannet*) , near Londonderry in Northern Ireland. I was to be attached to a course of Australian pilots on the anti-submarine training course. On completion of the course they were destined to fly the new Gannet twin propeller, twin-engined turbo jet. These aircraft had been purchased by the Australians to equip their carrier, HMS *Melbourne*. On completion of their training at Eglinton, the Australian pilots were to be appointed to HMS *Seahawk*, Culdrose in Cornwall to convert and 'work up' on the Gannet prior to their return to Australia. For the moment though, we all had to learn the anti-submarine trade on the ageing Firefly. This aircraft had proved a very useful tool in the Second World War and gave a good account of itself in the more recent Korean War. The Marks 5 and 6 were now being used to train pilots in anti-submarine procedures in anticipation of the formation of operational Gannet squadrons in the Royal Navy in the following months

Trundling up the Antrim coast to join Eglinton on a dull winter's day, the old steam locomotive huffed and puffed its way up from Belfast. As we approached the airfield, the railway wound around the edge of Lough Foyle towards Londonderry. Firstly, we passed the RAF Ballykelly airfield with its Shackleton anti-submarine long-range patrol aircraft, developed from the famous Lancaster, then we rattled on very, very, slowly along the edge of large mud banks of the lough, exposed by the falling tide. Canted at all angles in the mud were poles with lights on them. I was soon to find they were the almost derelict remains of the approach lights to Eglinton's main runway. Just short of touchdown, we passed the very recent wreck of a Firefly, partly buried in the mud just off the end of the runway. In a thoughtful frame of mind, I had arrived at my next home. It seemed very different from the efficient newness of Lossiemouth.

In fact, Eglinton was a cosy little place. Split by the main road to Londonderry, its accommodation was on the inland side, with the airfield next to the lough. All the accommodation blocks were prefabricated wooden buildings. Nothing could have changed much since the station's wartime construction; I felt I was entering a time warp. Later, I even discovered old wartime Barracuda aircraft mouldering away in a deserted part of the airfield.

I found the wardroom and checked in with my joining instructions. I was taken to my cabin and in no time at all met my boisterous neighbours, the Australians, and a few Royal Navy pilots, like me, attached to the course for conversion. I was delighted to find them a good humoured, easy-going group who, like our short service officers, had come from all walks of life. Their senior officer was a regular Royal Australian Navy lieutenant, presumably destined for command of a squadron. After the long weary journey, I settled into my cabin, going to bed in a contented frame of mind. I felt as if this was the right place for me. I was going to enjoy life as an anti-submarine pilot.

The next day the assorted new pilots assembled at 737 Squadron's group of wooden buildings that had served as administration, flight offices and crew rooms for various naval squadrons during and since the war. There we made our acquaintance with the instructors and learned of the programme ahead. On the hard standing outside, lined up and waiting, were ten or so Firefly Mark 5s and 6s in duck egg and sea grey operational livery. With them was a single, silver, dual seat Mark

1 trainer. Even at distance they looked formidable beasts and in the previous twenty-four hours we had all been well briefed on the real or imagined vices that these aircraft had waiting for the unwary pilot. We already knew that the wreck at the end of the runway had been fatal for the Canadian student on the previous course. Late on his final approach he had found himself too low, and set to land in the shallows, short of the runway. Alarmed, he slammed open his throttle in an attempt to overshoot. The Firefly was infamous for its torque stall, and the sudden increase of power as the throttle was rapidly opened caused the Firefly to flick roll around its propeller, crashing into the lough mud. This, we were told, was a common pilot error on deck landing with this powerful aircraft. We listened intently, with a certain amount of foreboding, the English members of the course hoping that the delivery of the incoming Gannet would not be long delayed.

A day to settle in and collect the *Pilot's Notes*; the usual small pocket book of specifications and techniques for flying the Firefly. Later there was a chance to sit in the cockpit and check out the controls with an attendant instructor alongside, pointing out salient controls and instruments. To the casual observer, an aircraft cockpit seems confusingly full of incomprehensible controls and instrument dials. In fact the pilot needs only to know initially the location of the many that he will never use, until they are required for a specific task. The 'primary' instruments are fortunately few and relate to the control of the engine such as engine revolutions, oil pressure and temperature, and the instruments required for flight control. In a very short time a pilot learns to scan his instruments as automatically as the scanning he does outside the aircraft, to check the skies around him. He can soon note a malfunction, much as a car driver scans his instrument panel and his mirrors.

I realized that, if it would let me, I could enjoy this aircraft. The single seat was personal; it was mine. I think that, subconsciously, I had always disliked the side-by-side seating of the previous training aircraft, the Vampire; it was probably due to an only child's reluctance to share its toys.

Brian Allen on joining the Royal Navy as a Short Commission Aviation Cadet.

A de Haviland Vampire T22.

A Fairey Firefly Mk 5 used for anti-submarine training.

The author at RNAS Eglinton in 1956.

The Fairey Firely Mk 7.

HMS *Albion* in 1960.

Brian Allen landing on HMS *Albion* during 1956.

The Fairey Gannet AS1 seen at RNAS Culdrose in 1956. The port wing is seen folded and the 'diamond' pattern on the fuselage indicates the footholds for the pilot's perilous climb to the cockpit.

The author in tropical rig when serving on *Albion* in 1956.

A Grumman Avenger.

A Westland
Whirlwind Mk 7
anti-submarine
helicopter.

The Saunders Roe P 531,
prototype of the Navy
Wasp and army Scout
production helicopters.

The Sikorsky S51 Dragonfly search and rescue helicopter.

The Hiller basic training helicopter.

That night after dinner and a companionable drink or two with the other members of the course, most of us retired early to our cabins to try and memorize the most important paragraphs in the *Pilot's Notes*. The next day would see the anti-submarine course start in earnest. It was back with too long nacelles, restricted vision and tail wheels. For the time being, I was finished with jets and my flying would be mostly within sight of land or sea.

My logbook states that on 11 January 1955, Lieutenant Commander Sandy Sinclair took me for my first familiarization flight in the Mk. 1 trainer. I sat in the pilot's seat whilst he sat someway back behind me in the instructor's position. With the extremely long Rolls-Royce Griffon engine stretching out in front of me some twelve feet or more, I wondered how he could have any forward view at all. On take-off, at a safe height, Sandy demonstrated the controls and gave me control. The aircraft was very comfortable to fly, responsive and apparently docile. Landing was no problem because, luckily, Sandy was at the controls. It was decidedly different from anything I had experienced before. With the long engine a conventional three point landing offered absolutely no forward visibility, and one had to quickly adapt to other references to the side to maintain a straight line when on the ground or, as when taxiing, the Firefly was weaved left and right like an inebriated old lady in order to get a view forward.

After about four hours' dual, I went solo and quickly bonded with this lovely aeroplane, my first operational aircraft.

On returning from a sortie you could descend into the circuit, with throttle fully back, the engine producing a wonderfully satisfying burbling, crackling, popping sound like a very powerful motor cycle. With landing checks completed you turned onto the final approach with power back on. Getting rapidly closer, the muddy shore of the lough slid by underneath, finally getting closer to touch down, the wrecked Firefly forlornly reminding you of your vulnerability passed underneath, warning you to 'watch out'. The airfield fence and runway threshold then flashed underneath your wheels; close the throttle, ease back the control column and you were down. Wonderful! I felt a sense of arrival and a large measure of relief. Although there was still a long way to go, I felt I was at last, officially a naval pilot, flying an operational naval aircraft

I have to confess that later, I usually adopted a main wheels only landing that gave a far better view over the nose. It was frowned upon by the instructors as slightly infra dig because it was a risky, even impossible way to catch a wire on a carrier. As I anticipated that I would be flying a Gannet, with a nose wheel and a nose down landing technique when landing on the deck, I was not too worried.

As I was to find out within a year or so, fate is a very fickle lady indeed, and I had good cause to regret not practising tail wheel down, three-point landings much more assiduously.

In the air you had excellent all round visibility aided by a useful rear view mirror so that you were not blind to any approach from behind. This was an operational aircraft of the Fleet Air Arm and together with the American built Grumman Avenger, was the mainstay of the fighter/bomber or anti-submarine force up to that date, although they were both in the process of being phased out in favour of the new Fairy Gannet. Naturally we flew alone, or with an instructor in the trainer. We were always briefed before sorties and I felt that at last I was in the right environment for me. The first 10,000 feet or so above the earth held all the interest and exhilaration for me.

The summer progressed with all of us happily firing rockets and dropping bombs on rubber dinghy targets at Minearny and Magilligan ranges, depth charging towed targets at sea and, thankfully only once, a RATOG take-off.

The RATOG device consisted of two large rockets fitted just behind the cockpit on either side of the fuselage. The objective was to get the aircraft airborne in a short distance in light wind conditions. The procedure was to line up on the runway ready to take-off with full flap, apply power, apprehensively hold your breath and push the little red button marked RATOG on the control column. After that, there was no going back. There was a moment of indecision before it fired and then with an almighty slam in the back you were on your way. With flames and smoke pouring from the rockets, the aircraft raced down the runway and, in very short time, was hurled into the air. Everything then went quiet as the rockets died out. The aircraft seemed to hang in the air and time stood still, but the silence was comparative as the good old Griffon was still going strong. You could then climb away wondering at the initiative that could invent something like RATOG. I was to find that only the catapult on the carrier compared in fright factor. When I watch a launch nowadays from Cape Canaveral, I relive the trepidation of a RATOG take-off as the lift-off, with its irresistible power, is blotted out by smoke.

The anti–submarine course rolled on. The Australians were a great bunch, always in a good humour and I became very attached to them, relishing the thought that, on completion of our time at Eglinton, there was a good chance of going to Cornwall together to make up our respective squadrons.

At this stage of training, two more of the English pilots were taken off the course. As can be imagined, at this stage, a great deal of money has gone into their training. The decision to 'chop' aircrew is not taken lightly. It is only a potentially fatal inability to cope in training with what was nearing completion to an operational qualification that led to that dreaded decision. To get this far and then fall must have been extremely disappointing. Fortunately I went on to complete the course on 29 March 1955 and was appointed to 765 Squadron, RNAS Culdrose, to await the commissioning of 825 Squadron, my first front line appointment, and the delivery of their new Gannets. It was with regret that I had finished with the Firefly, or so I thought. At least I had qualified as an operational pilot and was now ready to continue training with a squadron. We had our farewell party in the wardroom, thanked the patient instructors and agreed to meet up at Culdrose. I caught the train to rattle through the pretty County Down countryside to Belfast, and the ferry to Liverpool for a brief stay at Selsdon before going on to HMS *Seahawk* in Cornwall.

Chapter 6

You are Commanded to Proceed

I received my official instructions from the Admiralty, 'You are appointed to 825 Squadron and are to join that squadron at Royal Naval Air station HMS *Seahawk*, Culdrose. You are commanded to proceed to HMS *Seahawk* for attachment to 765 Squadron until the commissioning of said 825 Squadron.'

Towards the end of April 1955, after returning to England and spending a few days with my wife, I arrived at HMS *Seahawk*, RNAS Culdrose, near Helston in Cornwall. The Australians were already there and their squadron had formed, patiently awaiting the delivery of their Fairey Gannets AS Mk. 1. For Royal Navy personnel, 765 Squadron was a holding squadron in which aircrew assembled until their front line squadron was formed up and equipped with its own aircraft. We pilots were gathering in 765 to keep in flying practice until the Gannets, observers and telegraphists could join us later. We were also short of the senior members of the squadron, including the commanding officer.

Looking out of the crew room window, I was surprised to see a line of very large Firefly Mk 7s on the hard standing. I was soon informed that they were ours to use, until the Gannets arrived, so I had not quite finished with the Firefly after all. On the arrival of the new commanding officer, Lieutenant Commander 'Johnny' Johnson and the other senior members, we would be melded into the crews that would stay together when the three-man Gannet aircraft arrived in the next few weeks. In the meantime out there, for us to play with, the Firefly 7s quietly waited.

This was to be the first time I had just been issued with *Pilot's Notes* and left to get on with it without a dual sortie to familiarize with the aircraft. It all felt rather professional and, when I stood by the Mk 7, scary but exhilarating. The plane was huge, the latest mark of Firefly, powered as ever by the Rolls-Royce Griffon engine. Delayed by various problems, it had been the last development of the Firefly family, firstly too late completing its trials and then deemed too heavy to serve in the carriers, it had limited production and been superseded by the Gannet as the front line choice for carrier operations. It had all the familiar lines of the Firefly family and with its two rear seats, had been used for observer training, restricted to flying only from land bases.

For a more extensive knowledge of the whole of the fine Firefly clan, I can recommend the *Firefly, In the Cockpit* series 4, by Lieutenant Commander J.G.S. Norman, RN.

On 22 April I climbed up the wing root to clamber into the cockpit for my first flight. Safely belted in, looking at the controls, it all looked very similar to earlier models. After carrying out the now familiar cockpit checks, I selected the Coffman starter, (rather like a six-gun) fitted to the side of the engine and fired the cartridge. With a loud hiss and a cloud of smoke, the propeller turned and the engine thankfully fired into action. It was always reassuring to start an engine at first attempt in front of the critical eyes of your ground crew. It gave them the impression that you knew what you were doing and were not ill-treating their aircraft. Once in the air the Mk. 7 behaved very much like its siblings. It was a joy to fly and, during that glorious summer, gave many hours of pleasure as I flew around the Cornish peninsula trying to improve my flying skills, as few and embryonic as they were. My wife decided that she would like to join me at Culdrose for whatever time was left to us before 825 Squadron embarked. A married quarter, available for a young officer without children was out of the question, so we moved into rooms at St Keverne. For a month or two I hurtled across the Lizard in our little Morris Eight. Then we were lucky enough to find a small cottage to rent at Nancegollan, a hamlet just the other side of Helston from Culdrose. We still maintained our small flat in Selsdon as we knew the idyllic life in Cornwall could not last more than a few months. It was a perfect, relaxing few months. The spring developed into a beautiful summer and we flew daytime sorties around the Cornish coast, often carrying eager ground crew who seldom had the chance to see just what their charges did after taking-off from the airfield. We indulged them by flying low, thundering round the cliffs of west Cornwall at below cliff height with holidaymakers above us snapping away on their cameras. They were delightful carefree days. We were unable to carry out the much requested aerobatics. The Mk. 7 was limited to straight and level flight as violent manoeuvre would, it was thought, overstress the wings of the heavy machine. Rumour had it that there were cracks in the main spar of the wings, safe enough at present but possibly catastrophic if we abused the aircraft and indulged in violent aerobatics. Consequently we flew with a gentle touch, as smoothly as our limited experience allowed. After flying, I could race home to Nancegollan and enjoy all the domestic pleasures that had, to date, been limited by our separation as I completed my training courses. We wandered happily around the coastal villages of Cornwall, familiar ground, as it had been our regular holiday venue for several years as teenagers. Frequently, members of the Australian squadron accompanied us on these explorations and I had the pleasure of showing some of them that, in Australia, they didn't have the monopoly on big sharks during boat trips out of Mevagissey. There had been students on the earlier courses who were accompanied by their families while training but it was not encouraged and I personally felt it would have been a distraction. So now it was wonderful to be together at last and struggle with the odd dilapidated furnishings and antique equipment found in rented accommodation. Little did we know that this weird, nomadic lifestyle would continue until 1958, when we were allocated our first married quarter. MQs as they were called, were allocated on a points system and it was a bitter bone of contention that a young married officer stood little chance of a married quarter as he was always being leap-frogged by new officers joining the station long after him, with children and other point scoring assets, often, just as he had reached the top of the list. Squadron aircrew were not considered to be an established part of the land base and, equally disappointing, a squadron would embark on a carrier and the unfortunate officer would be removed from the list. Luckily, having the apartment in Selsdon, we maintained a permanent refuge. I was somewhat amused to hear in the later years, when much more money was available and mortgages easily obtained, that young officers, knowing that only a few carriers were in service, were buying their own property near air stations at which they knew that they would spend their disembarked periods, leaving MQs unoccupied and unwanted. The Admiralty tried to redress the situation by ordering them into quarters. My sympathies lay with the young officers.

Meanwhile we eagerly awaited the new Gannet as the pilot strength built up in 765. Finally the commanding officer and other senior officers joined us and the embryonic squadron began to take shape as the summer faded. We still kept up flying in the Fireflies, but we were invited to the Armstrong Siddeley works where our new machines were in their final preparations for delivery. It was a very interesting introduction to the aircraft that heralded a whole new era of anti–submarine operations. The aircraft could provide a complete package of anti-submarine and other air-sea attack weaponry. For detection of targets, a range of directional and passive sono-buoys could be carried with a mix of homing torpedo and depth charges in its bomb bay. Bombs also were part of the internal contents and, in a more peaceful environment, the bomb bay could be used for all sorts of storage – carrying kit and mail being the most common and very popular role. In addition an attack could be prosecuted using externally mounted rockets on wing rails. Radar, in a retractable 'dustbin' radome provided a useful but fairly short-range search and navigation facility. The Double Mamba turbo-jet engines presented a new concept of engine handling to us, with their constant speed independent units. It was unbelievable that two such small engines could power the huge aircraft; the weight was well over 10 tons when laden. The view from every cockpit was a joy after the Firefly. Armstrong Siddeley gave us a very good tour and they were obviously proud of their new product. We returned to Culdrose happy with what we had seen and doubly anxious to get our hands on the Gannet.

At Culdrose in 1955 we busied ourselves with ground duties in preparation for the impending visit of the Mk 1 Gannet trainer due to arrive any day to familiarize us with the new Gannets. We moved across to the hangar and offices that were designated to 825 Squadron but still shared a hard standing with 765. This meant that when they arrived, the new aircraft would stand alongside the Fireflies. At the time I paid it no heed but soon after we became a front line unit I, personally, discovered the reason for this cosy arrangement. The new offices and crew rooms soon became home to the virtually complete squadron and everyone began to settle in and take their place in the new regime. Lieutenant Commander 'Johnny' Johnson was a very quiet person and without fuss began to meld the individual aircrew into the unit he was to command. We were a pretty mixed bag of newly qualified observers and relatively inexperienced pilots such as me, together with several longer serving pilots and observers to bolster our confidence with their expertise. I was surprised to find what were called 're-tread' pilots amongst these older pilots. They were ex-FAA pilots who had rejoined the service after leaving at the end of the war and the later Korean conflict. Many had been unable to settle again in civilian life, and had applied to come back into the fold. One of these, now in 825, was Dennis Grimes, a small, quietly spoken man, probably in his forties. He could be found smoking a cigarette at the end of a long holder when at rest in the crew room, as he frequently was. He had previously flown Seafires in the last days of the war and his tales of deck-landing those skittish aircraft made very interesting chats when the weather was bad enough to prevent flying and we had to wait impatiently in the crew room. I was destined to go with him to our next appointment, when 825 de-commissioned in August 1956 on its return from the only embarkation of this phase of a famous squadron's service. An extremely entertaining history of the Fairey Gannet can be found in the *From the Cockpit Series, Gannet* by Simon Askins.

I must confess that I liked the Gannet, but after reading its full history in *Gannet*, I was amazed to discover how dangerous it proved to be and how many serious faults were discovered during its operational life. I must have been incredibly lucky, as were the other members of the squadron. In the year or so that I flew the Gannet I can remember only one wheels-up landing caused by a hydraulic fault, and one instance of a closed down engine failing to re-light.

Despite strict instructions not to attempt to aerobat the 10-ton monster, I can also remember an instance when the Gannet demonstrated its considerable, if unexpected, agility. One evening there was a twilight launch at Culdrose for night flying. The dying evening sun softly lit a cloudless sky and the first Gannet sortie had taken off some time before. At this point commander (air) sauntered into the control tower to check on the proceedings. He casually glanced towards the setting sun beyond Lands End and high in the sky saw a solitary Gannet carrying out an unmistakeable barrel–roll. Apoplectic, he whirled round, demanding to know the offending pilot's name and, saw to the east, a looping Gannet. There was an immediate re-call of all aircraft and an attempt to locate the guilty parties ensued. I do not think any official action was taken or even if the offenders were identified. Nothing more was said about the adventurous but foolhardy incident. I do know, however, that one of the culprits went on to become a qualified Empire test pilot, a prestigious position in aviation circles.

Chapter 7

Here Come the Big, Fat Faireys

Within weeks the Gannets started to arrive, and 5 July 1955 saw my first dual flight in the newly arrived aircraft. By now, the observers and squadron ground crew were joining us.

Two separate Armstrong-Siddeley Mamba engines, mounted side by side, each driving a single contra-rotating propeller, powered the Fairey Gannet. This gave it a twin-engined performance with a single engined configuration. By naval standards of the time the aircraft was huge and access was by climbing up the side using an extending ladder and footholds up the side of the fuselage. It was rather like rock climbing and absolutely essential to start off with the correct foot, or embarrassingly, you found yourself twenty feet up, clinging on, between the cockpit and propellers, with a right leg waving about in space near the propellers and unable to get into the cockpit.

In truth the Gannet looked a rather ungainly bird and would never win any beauty competition, but it had a sense of purpose and gave the impression that it could do the job for which it was built. To us, it was new, and we were the second squadron to form with the aircraft, so we were eager to start flying it. I know that there were critics of the Gannet and its performance but I found it a very comfortable flight and it gave me great pleasure to fly it. Someone had named it the 'gentleman's aircraft' and I wholeheartedly agree with whoever made that observation.

With other squadron aircrew and ground crew arriving nearly every day, the new 825 now formed together and was ready to be commissioned as a squadron. My observer was a newly qualified sub-lieutenant, Alan Jennings. He had apparently become bored with his chosen career as an architect and with National Service looming he had taken a sabbatical four-year short service commission as an observer, which I thought very brave. Our telegraphist for the rearmost cockpit was to be decided later.

By this time I had taken several familiarization solo trips in the Gannet to get to know the aircraft before being unleashed on an unsuspecting crew who relied on me to get them back alive. I have never understood how someone can continually entrust his life to some other person; a pilot was the only position for me. I found the Gannet to be virtually without vice and docile. A very smooth ride and excellent visibility appealed to me. Whilst easy to fly, it was agile enough to be interesting, although it had a single-engined performance for economical general purpose flying, a single-engined landing needed a long and careful approach to a long runway. I did not ever hear of a single-engined deck landing and it would have been a desperate pilot who attempted one. However, I thought it a well-planned successor to the Firefly although there were limitations; the American Grumman Tracker aircraft in service with the US Navy at the time seemed a much better all-purpose anti-submarine package.

Quickly the Squadron built up and we were commissioned at the end of June. While waiting for our full complement of Gannets, we still had access to the Mk 7 Fireflies. But, of course, we were now so keen to get as many hours as possible on the Gannet, that we rarely used them, clamouring instead to get our hands on the new bird.

Sitting in the crew room one fine day, eagerly awaiting my turn to fly the new plane, the senior pilot looked in and said he had a job for me. I was to fly the senior observer to the Fairey plant at White Waltham for an urgent conference. I jumped at the chance, as this would be an interesting way to get several hours in my logbook. He then dashed my hopes by saying that, as there were no Gannets to spare, I was to take a Mk 7 Firefly. I hadn't flown the Firefly for about ten weeks or so and never thought I would have to fly it again. My brain was full of details about the Gannet and now I had to fly the big Firefly to a small grass field somewhere west of London at short notice. My enthusiasm dwindled as I made hurried arrangements to file some sort of flight plan while Pete Woolings, my passenger, waited somewhat impatiently. He climbed into his cockpit with far more confidence than I did into mine.

As we crossed southern England the weather deteriorated with low cloud and rain dramatically reducing visibility. Pete seemed disinclined to navigate and the Fairey company airfield could only offer very basic aids to landing. I gingerly let down through cloud and was delighted to break through and become visual with the ground at about 600 feet, in drizzle, hoping I was somewhere in the vicinity of Fairey's field at White Waltham. What luck! Fairey's field lay dead ahead, in the murk, with the factory buildings, now visible, to one side. Feeling smugly pleased with my successful navigation, I prepared to land and made my approach. Conversation with the air traffic control at White Waltham had been minimal other than to establish wind direction and the fact that there were no other aircraft stupid enough to be up in this weather. As I approached on finals at about 300 feet I noticed that the field was covered with football goal posts. Levelling off to overshoot, but careful not to pullback up into the cloud, we skated over what was very obviously a sports ground. The factory buildings at the side declared, in big letters, on the roof, that it was the Huntley and Palmers biscuit factory. It dawned on me that they must have had this problem before. At least, I now knew where I was. The next large field, now looming ahead in the mist, was Fairey's and I was virtually there. I landed with a great deal of relief, bumping over the grass to an obscure corner of the field. Pete climbed down with a nod and drove off in a car that had arrived to collect him and I was left in the cockpit, hood firmly closed, reliving our last horrifying few minutes. During this, somewhat alarming, event, Pete hadn't said a word, so neither did

I, and to this day he knows nothing of how close he came to having unlimited biscuits with his morning coffee. An hour or so later, Pete returned and climbed silently into his cockpit. The damp wait had done nothing to sharpen my wits and I stupidly used an entire magazine of starter cartridges trying to start the engine, having omitted to switch on the essential magneto switches. My mood did not improve when the Fairey ground crew claimed complete ignorance of reloading the Coffman starter. I had to climb out in the rain to reload the breech myself. Having started successfully, we flew back in the late evening. As dusk was falling with the runway lights on, I landed back at Culdrose after a hectic day, with the silent Pete. It was to be my last flight in the Firefly, and my first and only night flight in the Mk 7. I learned a lot that day. Mostly about careful planning and also that by taking an unnecessary risk, the risk itself is usually greatly increased. I now knew, as well, how to reload the Coffman starter breech.

Our training proceeded apace as we awaited news of our future as a squadron. We knew that front line squadrons usually embarked in a carrier when 'worked up', and we hoped for an exotic cruise to some distant shores. When, eventually the news filtered down, we were delighted to find that we were to embark in HMS *Albion*, a small light fleet carrier, to sail with her sister ship *Centaur* to the Far East.

We settled down to working up with the Gannet and a full programme kept us busy with anti-submarine exercises that included dropping a homing torpedo on a hapless submerged submarine, specially padded for what I thought must be very dispiriting experience for the unfortunate crew. Time after time they saw us approach and the torpedo drop. They then had to hear its chattering progress until, with a deafening clunk, it logged their doom in a real attack scenario. To appreciate the team aspects of sub-hunting, we flew in small groups of two or three aircraft, to Eglinton for the joint anti-submarine training course at HMS *Sea Eagle*, Londonderry. This was a fascinating course developed to show all aspects of operations against submarines to everyone in the considerably mixed team of sub-hunters. The Navy, with its frigates using large, advanced sonar sets to detect and depth charges to drop over the stern or discharge to the side or a mortar system to fire ahead of the ship, depending on the location and attack direction.

The RAF Shackleton bombers of Coastal Command carried out long sea patrols from land and were equipped to search with sound detection gear and radar in order to attack with bombs and depth charges and, because of their size and speed, less commonly with rocket or torpedo. We in the more agile aircraft could also hunt from carriers with directional sonar buoys that would actually give a bearing on the target or passive sonar buoys that were dropped as a pattern, with the observer plotting his interpretation of signals to position the target for attack.

The course at Londonderry was aimed at all three services associating in the common cause, appreciating specific problems and to improve communication so that all anti-submarine action could be coordinated. To this end teams from each service gathered at *Sea Eagle* for fourteen days of simulated actions that were carried out in realistic conditions. There was even a mock up of a frigate's bridge and operations room that actually moved to simulate the motion at sea. It was so like the real thing, especially in night actions, that seasickness was not unknown amongst aircrew acting as the naval team during a 'game' that could last four hours or more. Surrounding the room were cabins equipped as the different aircraft would be, and all were linked by a common communication system. It impressed on all of us the need for constant liaison and accurate communication in prosecuting a joint attack on an ever-elusive submarine. Exercises at sea with live submarines and frigates enabled us to log some useful hours in the air and remind the submariners of what they already knew – hostile aircraft are bad news.

We returned to Culdrose elated by our 'games'. The next big event would be attempting to land on a deck for the first time, after a few more weeks practice with the submarine, honing the skills that we had obtained at Londonderry. In spite of everything, the advantage remained with the submarine, and I believe it still does. The sub-hunters success still depends on the accurate prosecution of that first nebulous contact. Keeping a submarine submerged and denied visual contact with its target is usually as much as can be achieved.

Chapter 8

825 Squadron – The First Commission

Flying training with the Gannet continued apace with exercises perfecting the hunting skills of the observers and telegraphists involving real submarines, and the subsequent bombing skills for me. The submariners were very tolerant of our efforts to prove their vulnerability. First we would drop a pattern of sono-buoys which, when immersed, would send back any sounds made by the submerged boat with a bearing. This would be compared with other bearings from other buoys in the pattern and the position of the target could be calculated. Instructed by the observer, I would open the bomb doors and fly along his chosen attack path dropping small grenades when he reckoned we were over the submarine. This sounds a lot easier than it actually was, but in these somewhat artificial conditions, I occasionally saw the submerged target and tried to straddle it with a couple of my tiny bombs.

Debriefings were often heated affairs, with the submariners disputing that we had been anywhere near them, with us just as confident that we had a 'kill'. Once, with everything down, wheels, flaps and bomb doors open, and going as slowly as I could, we circled a submerged boat, dropping bombs by his conning tower every time we passed. The worried captain later asked how we had done this. I cheerfully explained that I could

easily see his submerged boat, because he had fitted a smart
white rubber decking on his conning tower bridge, and I could
clearly spot it under the water. I hope that he learned a lesson and
forgave us for any headaches, or frustration, suffered by the
barrage of bombs. In addition to making our own attacks, by
using our own sonar buoy screen, we could plot the underwater
submarine and we could then also direct anti-submarine frigates
onto the target or call in another aircraft to drop depth charges
or a homing torpedo in a simulated attack. I appreciate that these
exercises suggest that once an aircraft appears, the submarine is
doomed but they were designed only to perfect or develop
techniques for aircrew and were completely unrealistic. The
history of anti-submarine warfare shows that many hundreds,
perhaps thousands, of hours of patrolling are required by air and
sea units to achieve even a contact with a submarine, let alone an
attack. In war it could have taken years before an aircrew
actually spotted an enemy submarine. The advantage still lies to
a great extent with the submariner. Nevertheless, most
submariners have a healthy respect for any aircraft they see on
their periscopes or on their radar and will avoid contact if at all
possible. By denying them access to position themselves for an
attack, aircrew have achieved their objective without ever
knowing that they have done so.

The year passed with one very sad event, when a particular
Australian friend, in one of their Gannets, mysteriously crashed
and was lost off the Isle of Wight. Jim Van Gelder, a typical
craggy, outspoken but good natured 'Aussie', and I had explored
Cornwall and the Lake District together with my wife and his
girlfriend and I felt his loss keenly, especially as there was no call
from the aircraft indicating trouble and no obvious cause to
explain the accident.

I found the Gannet to be a very smooth ride without any
discernable vices. With a single engine performance, if one engine
failed, there was always a good chance of at least getting back,

and as I found later, it deck landed like a dream. Before the Gannet single engined aircraft were frequently lost and, whilst not full of thrills, she was an impeccable lady and I looked forward to a long association. I was to find later that again fate had a very different future mapped out and waiting for me.

Towards the end of 1955, we were informed that we would be embarking on HMS *Albion* for a commission to the Far East in January 1956. This caused great excitement as, with increasing limitations on expenditure, a Mediterranean cruise was the more normal operating theatre for carriers in those ever more stringent times.

The art of deck landing was now the main topic of conversation with the pilots. Our few old and bold pilots, as well as the newly fledged, had to learn the new techniques with the new deck mirror landing aid and the new Gannet. Luckily the main runway at Culdrose had one of these wondrous mirrors fitted and from now on every landing was completed with reference to the mirror.

The mirror and the angled deck had made dramatic improvements to the safety aspects of deck landing. The mirror meant that accurate flying using the datum of green and white glide path lights would always land the plane in amongst the arrester wires. It was, like most inventions, a simple use of known facts about mirrors. A concave mirror was tilted to reflect a beam of light at an angle, in this case 3 degrees, and stabilized to maintain the angle despite the ship's motion, with fixed bars of green lights either side providing a datum and the whole apparatus installed by the side of a selected wire. It provided the approaching pilot with a visual 3 degree flight path to that particular wire when the white and green lights were kept in alignment. It was usually set up with No. 3 wire, a middle wire, which meant that wires either side could also engage the hook on the aircraft if a slightly erratic landing was made by a pilot and No. 3 wire was missed. The pilot, on approach, was required to keep the white light in the mirror aligned with the green datum lights. If the white light was too high and the pilot did not make any adjustment to the descent path, he would miss the wires and have to go round again for another attempt. With the white light too low, a far more dangerous situation was developing. The aircraft was too low and a continued approach would result in possibly striking the 'round-down' or worse, sinking too low and ultimately being confronted by the rapidly expanding rear end of the carrier. If for some reason, and there were many, a wire was not engaged, the angled deck provided a safe overshoot path, avoiding any aircraft parked forward on the flight deck. This event was known as a 'bolter'. Proof of the system's efficacy came when night deck landings were taking place. In darkness, the only reference available was the mirror and nearly every landing caught the most desired No. 3 wire.

The Gannet was an excellent aircraft for carrier landing. It was very stable but responsive, with a view forward that could not be bettered. A nose wheel made the essential flare at touchdown, to make a landing in an aircraft with a tail wheel, unnecessary. It needed only a steady approach with the white datum light in line with the bars of green lights on either side, and the Gannet would drive straight into the wires. The sensation of catching a wire and coming to an almost immediate halt from 80 knots or so was an altogether different matter. However, the relief at catching a wire was a great massage for the ego. I must stress that this in no way lessened the apprehension of the first ever, or indeed any, deck landings. They never failed to concentrate the mind.

On 6 October, I made my first approach to land on HMS *Bulwark*, in the English Channel. This moment, I think, is as momentous as any in a naval pilot's life. As I approached, and called the ship, it was butting through a choppy sea off the Isle of Wight. She looked every bit of what she was, a very small light fleet carrier. Flying control in the ship cleared me to join the circuit and make my first approach, as the deck was ready. I was grateful to find the landing deck a lot larger when close in and seen from the circuit. There was further relief after turning onto the downwind leg of the circuit approach, to complete, very carefully, my downwind checks, confirming that my wheels were down and that my flaps were fully extended. I turned onto the final approach and was delighted to see immediately the friendly green lights with a nice white light in the middle brightly shining up at me as promised. As I was cleared to start with 'bolter' touch and goes to gain confidence, I ensured that the arrester hook control indicated that it was firmly locked up. Down I went, careful to watch airspeed, and to check once again that wheels and flaps were locked down. Despite an inevitable apprehension, everything seemed to fall into place and the white light, with minor adjustments, remained steadfastly in line with the greens. After touching the deck with my wheels, I opened up the power to take-off again and go round again for another attempt. I was aware of the superstructure of the island with the other equipment on deck appearing perilously close on my right hand side as I sped down the deck and climbed away. After four more circuits and bolters, I was instructed by 'flyco', the flying control position in the 'island' of the carrier, to come around to complete a landing, the final initiation ritual for a carrier pilot. Once again I made the careful checks, this time to include lowering the arrester hook. This time I knew that speed was one of the vital factors of the approach, too fast and you could pull the hook out of the aircraft, too slow and you could sink below the flight deck level. Both mistakes could be embarrassing if not fatal. Luckily all went well and the Gannet obligingly thumped into the wires, like the lady she was, and I was strained against my straps, as we were brought to an abrupt halt from 85 knots in a few seconds. Disengaged from the wires, I was pushed back for a 'free' take-off using the whole deck to achieve a take-off speed for another circuit and landing. This was completed to everyone's apparent satisfaction and, with a jubilant farewell; I climbed away and returned to Culdrose.

I had made it. I was in a front line squadron of the Fleet Air Arm and had completed my first deck landings. I felt that Biggles would have been proud of me; every bit as amazed as I was, but still proud.

This was a purely personal emotion as there are few commendations for a job well done in the Royal Navy. Most achievements, when commented on, are greeted with a faintly astonished response, '...but that's what you are paid for'. Perhaps I should add that in those days flying pay was a heady £ 1.10 a day in today's currency.

The squadron continued its working up programme until, after Christmas leave, we embarked the Gannets on HMS *Albion* on 10 January 1956, as she proceeded down channel in the company of her sister ship HMS *Centaur*, outwards bound for the Far East. Nearly four years after joining the Fleet Air Arm, the fledgling had finally made it although, in truth, now embarked he felt the usual queasiness of seasickness. It vanished once in the aircraft and off the deck, which was a blessing, perhaps it is all in the mind.

Flying continued on almost a daily basis. The others who also joined the ship were a squadron of Hawker Seahawk day fighters, a squadron of de Havilland Sea Venom night fighters and last, but by no means least, a four plane flight of Douglas Skyraider airborne early warning aircraft. These aircraft were equipped with long range radar whose purpose was to fly patrols several hundred miles from the ship and relay their radar signals to the ship's operations room, extending the radar cover of *Albion* and giving early warning of any hostile approach.

While we pilots practised our deck landings and weapon delivery skills, the ship's operations staff worked with the observers to perfect their specialist skills. It was great fun for pilots to rocket and bomb a splash target towed astern of *Albion*. We were without a bombsight or other aid so any accuracy was purely accidental. We dived down on the moving target aiming the missile by sight of eye at a point ahead of the splash; it was amazing how skilled we became after a few runs.

During this period of 'working up' the squadron, yet another method of launching aircraft from carriers was introduced to the pilots who had never flown from the deck. It was to be my first catapult launch. The catapult was one of two tracks that extended back from the bow of the ship for several feet. At the end of the track is a shuttle that an aircraft is attached to by an especially strengthened steel wire strop. The catapult, using steam from the ship's engine room will, on demand, suddenly but progressively, propel the shuttle and aircraft from stationary to 100 knots in a few seconds, along the track and off over the bow so that as the strop drops away, the aircraft is hopefully airborne and climbing away. This, like landing on the deck, is an unforgettable event in a carrier pilot's life. Strapped firmly in your aircraft you taxied up to the bow where, marshalled by the deck crew, you were positioned on the catapult, where careful checks were made to ensure that the controls and trims were correctly set, both on the deck and in the aircraft. Once attached to the catapult shuttle shoe by the steel wire strop, you settled yourself in, staring at the empty sea ahead. When given the signal that all was well by the deck officer, the throttles were opened to full power. With the aircraft juddering and straining at the leash, you dropped your left hand, placing your fist behind the throttles to make sure the coming jolt from the catapult did not jerk them closed. This sudden impetus made it necessary to lodge the right elbow against your stomach to prevent your now jammed right hand inadvertently causing you to pull the control column backwards. Either mishap would have had disastrous consequences as you were thrown off the ship. The action of dropping the left hand indicated to the launch officer that you and the aircraft were prepared for a launch. At this signal the deck officer dropped his whirling flag. Once this happened, you were committed. Somewhere in the bowels of the ship, an unseen button was pushed and for a moment or two you could wonder if you had done all the right things before you were hurled off the bow to stagger away into flight; life stood still, the noise and apparent chaos of the deck had vanished behind you, and you fell into the familiar routine of selecting gear and flaps up and flying away.

We always took off with canopies open and locked so that if anything did go wrong, it would be easier to get out of the cockpit if, or when, we 'ditched'.

This method of taking off from a carrier is always used for the fighter aircraft but is useful for all types in calm, low wind conditions and I have read of launches from stationary ships in harbour, but it is not general practice, or for the faint hearted.

Our journey included brief stops in Gibraltar and Malta. Operating off Malta, the squadron suffered its first casualty. During a night flying practice, we were launched at dusk. The objective was to carry out some general flying until recalled individually to carry out our first deck landings at night. As this was a potentially dangerous exercise, without the need of observers or telegraphists, we flew solo. When Lieutenant Dick Reid was called in to rejoin the ship, there was no answer. An extensive air and sea search that night and the following day failed to find any trace of pilot or wreckage. He was a very popular officer, out of Dartmouth and with a permanent commission, and had been destined for a command in due course. There was nothing to indicate any emergency or any call from the pilot that suggested anything amiss. What happened remains yet another unsolved mystery.

A saddened ship sailed on for a courtesy call at Piraeus, Greece. This gave us a chance to visit the Acropolis and Parthenon in nearby Athens to brush up on our culture. From there we sailed to transit the Suez Canal and enter into the Red Sea. The canal, quite recently re-opened after the Suez conflict, was a new experience for many of us, and as we slowly made our way through, it was made obvious, by white robed Egyptians on the banks, that our presence was not exactly popular with the locals. Once clear of the canal, strewn with the wrecks of ships scuttled by the Egyptians, we made our way swiftly through the Red Sea to stop for a day or two at Aden, then in the early days of the ending of British occupancy.

We had been flying more or less continuously as we crossed the Med but it was a quiet passage for us in the Red Sea until I flew off to land and collect mail as we approached Aden, landing at RAF El Adem on 15 February. The mail collection flight was always a popular flight for the whole ship's crew, and the Gannet with the load capacity in the large bomb bay was an ideal workhorse for such occasions.

After leaving Aden we crossed the Indian Ocean to show the flag in India; our sister ship went on to Calcutta, whilst we visited Bombay. As we drew near our destination the Indian prime minister, Pandit Nehru came on board to witness a flying demonstration by the ship's aircraft. India was at that time concluding the purchase of their first carrier, the *Vikrant*, from the UK and I think his visit was to see just what India had bought with their hard-earned rupees.

The 825 Squadron contribution was to be a flypast salute to the prime minister. In close formation we ran up to the ship at low level using only one engine. This always impressed those unfamiliar with the Gannet as it seemed that, with the stopped propeller very visible, the whole flight was gliding past without power. As we passed it was planned to restart the stationary propeller in a formation relight. This procedure meant the pilot, at a command, had to smartly raise the high pressure fuel cock lever from the closed position at the bottom of its quadrant, up to the top to unfeather the propeller, wait until the propeller revs had reached the re-light speed and then press the re-light button on the lever. This, it was hoped, would give a demonstration of the aircraft's versatility and power. Unfortunately as I brought my lever up to the re-light position, it broke off in my hand before I could press the button. I was left holding the lever still, luckily, connected to the aircraft by the electrical wiring. This meant that everyone had two engines but me, and as we were in close formation with now rapidly differing speeds, I had to quickly break away from the formation to sort out the problem as single engine deck landings were considered impossible. I should explain that the lever's official title was the HP cock as in stopcock. In the heat of the moment, I called the formation leader to tell him, accurately but poorly phrased, that, 'my cock had broken off in my hand'. This drew an equally tactless reply, from an unknown wit, that it '...served me right, I shouldn't have been playing with it'. As all this R/T was possibly broadcast on the bridge for the benefit of our esteemed visitor and his staff, I can only hope that his command of English wasn't up to it. Anyway with a certain amount of luck I managed to get a thumbnail into a groove on the broken lever and lock it home. Pressing the re-light button on the dangling part fired up the silent engine and, with two engines, I landed on, somewhat relieved, with the rest of the Gannets.

Having completed, for me, an illuminating introduction to the East, we left Bombay with its masses, its obvious immense wealth and equally obvious grinding poverty, to continue on to what was then called Ceylon, now Sri Lanka. On the way we carried out various exercises with units of the Indian Navy to improve coordination between the two Navies. It meant a lot of flying under the direction of the Indian controllers. The intention was to prepare them for future operations with *Vikrant*, soon to arrive from UK. I found this interesting with quite a few language difficulties; none insurmountable, but time consuming. Any reader, who has had occasion to telephone a bank call centre or computer help line in Delhi, will appreciate the problem. I readily confess that if the Indian language had been the choice of communication the situation would have been totally chaotic.

After the hustle and bustle of Bombay with its crowds and frenetic activity, Ceylon seemed almost serene and deserted; a beautiful island, with verdant jungle and gleaming white buildings. As we drew near Colombo, we could see that it was, in fact, very nearly as busy as Bombay with frenetic traffic, but a somewhat calmer atmosphere prevailed. As in India, we were warmly welcomed and shown great hospitality with many opportunities to explore the country around Colombo. We, in turn, responded with parties on board and tours around the ship for our hosts. After a week or so we sailed on across the Indian Ocean into the Malacca straits, heading for a short stay at the Singapore dockyard, before heading north into the seas around Korea and Hong Kong. As we approached Singapore I was launched by catapult on the routine, but ever popular, mail run landing at the small naval airfield at Sembawang. The next day the whole squadron disembarked and landed at that delightful airfield with its wartime runways of metal mesh Summerfield tracking, to stay for a few days' relaxation and to carry out exercises with the forces there while *Albion* was in Singapore dockyard undergoing routine maintenance. At Sembawang we made our number with the Army Air Corps based there. They flew the little high wing Auster; an army spotter and communication aircraft, with a single engine. Their tales of adventures over, under and through the Malayan jungles filled us with awe and admiration. One epic story told was of the discovery of an Auster that had disappeared over the jungle en route from Singapore to Kuala Lumpur. Gurkhas found the wreckage at the base of a huge tree in dense jungle; the passenger was dead inside and one of the pilot's boots was on the wing. Despite an extensive search, he was never found but, when sitting on the wing alongside the boot, the would-be rescuers could clearly hear the road traffic on the highway only a matter of yards away from the wreck.

Repairs completed, HMS *Albion* sailed six days later and we rejoined as she sailed northwards to Hong Kong. On sailing, we were delighted to offer the army fliers the opportunity of claiming some deck landings in their logbooks. *Albion* had to slow down so that these tiny aircraft could catch up and put their wheels on the deck. It was mooted, by the amused naval aviators, that if *Albion* increased speed again, we could leave the Austers to fly away behind us; they only had to pull the control column back to get airborne.

The shopping, with the goods available in Singapore, had entranced me especially as, back at home, Britain was still suffering from austerity and shortages. As I had been informed that Hong Kong was 'twice as good but half the price' of Singapore, I was looking forward to that visit with great expectations.

On the passage up to Hong Kong we exercised with the French carrier, *La Fayette*. Their aircraft were supposed to find and strike *Albion*, while we reciprocated. I can remember one special moment when, in a formation of Gannets flying off the east coast of Malaya, we were bounced by a flight of Second World War French Chance-Vought Corsairs. They swept by us, unseen and unheard until it was far too late for us, and vanished into the haze. We were sitting ducks, and I thought with longing of how useful that rear mirror had been on the Firefly. Also obvious, was why the Japanese had called the Corsair 'Whispering Death'. During this passage the ship called in at Subic Bay in the Philippines to make our number with our American cousins. We were, as is usual, swamped with typical American hospitality at the huge airbase. When the Americans made reciprocal visits to *Albion*, they always expressed surprise at the smallness of the ship and amazement that the ugly Gannet actually flew. However, they conceded that, with its wings folded, it looked quaint.

We pressed on from Subic Bay with exercises nearly every day, with the military forces that were responsible for the peacekeeping guardianship of the area. Normally, only visiting aircraft carriers were available to them to hone their cooperation skills with aircraft.

At last, as we approached Hong Kong, the Gannets were launched to carry out a fly past of the city. This was my first view of that magical place. As we flew up the harbour entrance between Hong Kong and Kowloon I marvelled at skyscrapers edging the seafront with the old city crowding up the steep sides of Victoria and Wanchai. It was not quite so developed on the Kowloon side then, with the rapidly expanding main airport at the waterside already thrusting its main runway out into the mainstream. The notorious approach to this runway from the town end followed a glide path down the mountains at the back and finally landed on the runway between the dilapidated tenement blocks of downtown Kowloon. It seemed as if every landing would end up dragging in with it the long poles with lines of washed laundry that streamed from every window or balcony. Any overrun meant a wet walk back to the airfield.

It all presented an exciting vista to the new boy from Selsdon. I can assure you that Croydon came nowhere near. I couldn't wait to get ashore to sample the exotic atmosphere of the Orient.

After landing on, I hurried below to tell the unfortunate few who had stayed on board what I had seen, as we dressed in our white uniforms, to man the ship for entering harbour. The squadron's position, for the ceremony of entering, was across the front of the flight deck so we had a grand view of the approach to the harbour with its busy waterway alive with boats of all descriptions. Junks and sampans scuttled around in all directions, ignoring or avoiding the dozens of military and civilian ships of all nationalities that thronged the harbour. We slowly came to our mooring just offshore from the naval base, HMS *Tamar*. This shore base would provide our access to Hong Kong itself. We had hardly stopped when crowds of small boats anxiously trying to sell their wares or provide some real or imagined service, surrounded us. In no time at all there were boatloads of women dressed in black with coolie hats swarming up the sides of *Albion* slapping grey paint on her sides. The wardroom was full of Chinese agents offering tailoring, with 24-hour delivery, jewellery and oriental handicrafts of all kinds. With the help of 'old hands' we slipped into the way of bartering and soon I began wondering if I had missed my true vocation. I loved the friendly banter and negotiation essential to strike a price that suited all parties.

Hong Kong was an absolutely magical experience for me. HMS *Tamar* was situated on the waterfront in Wanchai, one of the many downtown areas of Hong Kong. Nothing was very far from the towering, glass skyscrapers of the commercial centre which dominated the whole area; the bustle was unbelievable. Trams, buses, taxis dodged the crowds of carts, rickshaws and pedestrians. The whole scene was like a speeded up film, you just had to join the frantic throng and be swept along hopefully, in the direction you wanted to go. For a bit of peace you could take the funicular tram up to Victoria peak and gaze in awe at the equally busy waterway and beyond Kowloon to the New Territories where the dour communist Chinese army glowered across the border in envy of their prosperous neighbours.

On a lighter note, there was an incident with the American carrier sharing Hong Kong's hospitality with us. As our visit drew to a close, a group of *Albion* sailors ashore had fraternally joined a group of Americans, to mutually enjoy the liquid refreshment so inexpensively available in the thousands of bars and clubs. One of the American sailors must have flaunted his latest tattoo, a huge American eagle emblazoned on his chest. Later, after a very happy 'run ashore' the assorted sailors weaved their way back to their respective ships. The next day there were indignant signals from the American authorities. Apparently our sailors had somehow persuaded the inebriated American sailor to overlay his 'eagle' with a vast Union Jack. There was no way he could remove his shirt in front of his shipmates. The two admirals talked it over and we heard no more. I often wondered what his wife said when he returned to the USA.

All too soon our stay was over and we sailed out to start the long voyage home. We repaid our hosts by staging a dramatic 'strike' on Kowloon, launching Seahawk fighters to carry it out. Sadly two of the Seahawks dived through cloud to make a low level run. Unfortunately the cloud was filled with a church on a hill and a civilian and the two pilots were lost; two more of my initial flying course friends would not make it back to home.

With the surviving aircraft safely recovered, the ship started the long journey home. Flying was very much reduced although my logbook shows a mail trip to Penang, a reconnaissance of the Addu Atoll in the Indian Ocean and then nothing very much until a flypast for the flag officer off Malta. With the bit between her teeth, the ship plunged on towards the next and final stage of the cruise for us. On the morning of 14 May 1956, the squadron launched for the last time; we disembarked for Culdrose while in the western approaches and, in formation, formally arrived home.

My first commission completed, I was more than happy to greet my wife, patiently waiting, in our designated hangar at

Culdrose. Later that day, I excitedly told her about my travels and made a solemn promise that one day I would take her to Hong Kong. Little did we know that it would take forty-five years to fulfil that promise. Needless to say, it had completely changed; it is now a vast commercial city, entwined with motorways, towering, vast skyscrapers and glossy shops. It was a great disappointment; one has to make a visit to Stanley to see a preserved microcosm of the old Hong Kong. Having said that, I fell in love with the Far East while on *Albion* and that feeling has never changed.

After a spot of leave, 825 flew a varied programme for the rest of June and August, while re-appointments were sorted out as the squadron was to disband. Towards the end of the month, one of the re-entrant, 'old and bold' pilots, Dennis Grimes, and myself were called into the CO's office. He announced that we had both been appointed to join 751 Squadron at RAF Watton, later to form ship's flight HMS *Warrior* at HMS *Daedalus*, Lee-on-Solent. Little did I know then that I was to go on one of the most interesting commissions of my naval career. I flew my last sortie in a Gannet on 7 August 1956. Then Dennis and I made our way to Norfolk to join 751 Squadron. We were looking forward to finding out just what the new appointment entailed, as it all seemed rather 'hush hush'. I was to find that fate was about to catch up with me and my 'sins' were to find me out.

We arrived at RAF Watton on a cold darkening evening in September and settled into the Officers' Mess. It was an old established RAF base with a standard, well spaced layout. The Mess had the typical features of all the previous accommodation that I had been in when hosted by the Air Force at Syerston. It didn't matter where you were, you could always find your way about an established RAF airfield.

Chapter 9

751 Squadron and HMS *Warrior*

After going through the required joining procedure on the station, we found the hangar and offices of 751 Squadron. Having made our introductions we sat down to discuss our future expectations. I was very surprised to find out that the UK intended to carry out three H-Bomb tests in the Pacific, based on Christmas Island and, furthermore, Dennis and I were to be part of the carrier support force. HMS *Warrior*, an ageing Second World War carrier was, for her last commission, to lead the naval task force. *Warrior* was tasked with providing air links between the target island Malden, and the main base, Christmas Island. Until the actual tests were completed, *Warrior* was to moor off Christmas Island and the helicopters of the ship's flight would provide communication links between ship and shore. There were about 400 miles of the Pacific separating Christmas and the target area, Malden Island. This area was to be prohibited to all vessels not involved with Operation Grapple.

It sounded very intriguing and very different from the usual front line squadron work. Lieutenant Commander Williams, CO of 751 Squadron, explained that the ship's flight would consist of six Whirlwind helicopters and three fixed-wing aircraft. Dennis and I would be the fixed-wing pilots although two of the other helicopter pilots would qualify on fixed-wing as well, to provide extra back-up. He then suggested we go with him to see the aircraft we would be flying. They were in the adjacent hangar. It all sounded very exciting.

Entering the hangar, my jaw dropped. There sat three ancient, large, lumpy Grumman Avengers in their deep blue livery, sitting squarely on a tail wheel. My fond thoughts of continuing to fly a modern aircraft with a nose wheel and good forward vision were dashed as I gazed up at the huge beasts in the hangar.

The CO continued with his briefing saying that, because aircraft carriers with the extra width caused by angled decks could not navigate the Panama canal, HMS *Warrior* with a straight deck had been chosen. Furthermore instead of the up-to-date mirror landing aid, to which I had grown accustomed in 825 Squadron, we would be required to carry out landings controlled by a batsman. I was stunned; I had never dreamed that I would ever have to land on a deck using methods that were now considered obsolete. Finally the CO told us that we should study *Pilot's Notes* and start familiarization flights the next day. With one more horrified look back at the tubby Avenger, it looked as if it well deserved its American nickname of 'Turkey', made at 'the Grumman Cast Iron Works'. I returned to the crew room in a very thoughtful frame of mind and started reading about the aircraft. Anyone who has watched film footage of the American war in the Pacific will have seen Avengers trundling down the decks of American carriers together with other carrier aircraft long consigned, with the carriers they flew from, to scrap yards or museums.

The next day the Avengers were waiting for Dennis and me on the hard standing. I climbed into mine and at once noted how comfortable it was in the pilot's cockpit. It was an American torpedo bomber developed for their Navy in the Second World War and saw a lot of service particularly in the Pacific where it was the mainstay bomber on US carriers. Large numbers had been sent under Lease-Lend arrangements to equip the Royal Navy. They were sturdy aircraft, a typical Grumman product, with a powerful radial Wright double-banked Cyclone engine and an enviable reputation for reliability and ruggedness. At this stage I did not know its range and fortunately never had to test it in earnest, but I would think that it could fly well in excess of the 400 miles we would expect of it. Like most American built aircraft it had an incredibly spacious cockpit with comfortable seating and, although of no interest to me, it even had an ashtray and, I believe, a cup-holder in an armrest. The instrument layout was somewhat different from those in the home produced product and, of course, lacking in some of the up-to-date, sophisticated aids I was used to in the Gannet, but nothing appeared to be too difficult to use, and it appealed to my romantic side to think that I was going to emulate those fliers of old. I started up the engine, and was comforted that it sounded like that old friend, the Harvard; a good throaty roar. I taxied round to take-off with my *Pilot's Notes* close at hand. After taking off at the recommended 80 knots, I climbed away for some general handling at a safe height, testing the manoeuvrability and stalling characteristics. The aircraft seemed to have few vices, handling well, but it obviously was not a 'sports' model; lumbering would be a better description. Satisfied, I returned to Watton for some 'touch and go' landings and a final landing to taxi back to dispersal, another name for the squadron hangar and hard standing area surrounding it. My introduction to my new steed had gone far better than I could have wished.

Back in the crew room, I considered events of the last few days. The task ahead seemed to be an extremely interesting one, unique in fact. The Avenger was very comfortable and appeared to be docile and without any unpleasant failings. It was true that a major hurdle lay ahead; I was yet to face a batsman assisted landing on a straight deck, in an aircraft that had a tail wheel. I felt it was a challenge I could thoroughly enjoy. I also felt privileged to be included in this historic operation. Between 7 September and 9 November, Dennis and I consolidated our flying on the Avenger. To Dennis, with his wartime experience of carrier flying, together with batted landings, the tasks ahead presented little or no difficulty. We were now joined by our designated batsman, Lieutenant Commander Sid Richardson, an ex Venom pilot, with many hours' flying experience; the appointment as deck landing officer was as new to him as the Avenger was to me. We were to practise the assisted dummy deck landings (ADDLs) on the runway at Watton, and to this end an outline deck had been painted on the runway. The carrier circuit height was at 400 feet and the technique required the pilot to make his final approach in a continuous curving descent to the runway, skating round in order to keep the batsman visible until the final commitment. His instructions were virtually mandatory, so by obeying the signalling instructions from the batsman from his position on the port side of the runway at the touchdown position, we were controlled all the way down to an arrival amongst the imaginary wires. If all went well and the approach was good, you would see his paddles stretched out sideways at his shoulder height, indicating that the aircraft looked set for a successful touchdown. As the aircraft came to the threshold and levelled to land, the batsman would give the 'cut throttle' signal and you closed the throttle and pulled the control column back as far as it would come. Again, if all was well, the Avenger would thump, tail down, on all three wheels, into the spot where wires would be on a carrier. It all sounds a great deal easier than it actually was. Nearly always there was some correction needed to the approach. If you were too high, the batsman's arms would rise up above shoulder height; if you needed to bank to line up, the arms would tilt, indicating the bank you needed to correct. After a while one got the hang of it, but I could never say I was good at batted landings, or controlled crashes as some cynics called them. I should also have practised more of those tail-down, three point landings in the Firefly at Eglinton. I was to find out all too soon how essential they were.

While at Watton, exercises were carried out testing the equipment in the rear positions that would be required in the Pacific, principally the navigation, radio and telegraphy aids. Apart from being told that our tasking was as communication aircraft, we had not been informed of any specific duties that would be expected of us. At present the operation seemed to be at a very much 'need to know' stage.

Early in November, Dennis and I travelled down to take up our original appointment. We joined ship's flight HMS *Warrior*, disembarked at HMS *Daedalus*, RNAS Lee-on-Solent, the same HMS *Daedalus* that I had last seen in 1952, when I attended the initial interviews. It felt as if a lot of water had flowed under the bridge since that day, four years before. I had certainly travelled about a bit.

Chapter 10

What are you doing at Christmas? Operation Grapple

The rest of the HMS *Warrior*'s ship's flight was already gathering at the base at Lee-on-Solent. As this was only a temporary base prior to embarkation, we were attached to the second line squadron operating out of Lee. It was the home of 705 Squadron, the small unit that was responsible for all helicopter training in the Royal Navy. This was long before the demand for crews to fly the anti-submarine made a much larger training unit necessary, although the idea of using helicopters in an offensive role was even then being considered. Larger, more powerful machines giving vastly increased load and range capabilities, were already flying in the United States and a far more expansive role was developing for the rotary-wing.

For the present 705 Squadron trained helicopter pilots who, when qualified, would provide the pilots for Search and Rescue flights on carriers and air stations, together with any specialized duty that required the unique abilities of the helicopter. There was little flying commitment at Lee so the airfield was quiet, with plenty of room for our small unit to settle in and work up towards the day when we would sail off in HMS *Warrior*. The Whirlwind helicopters and the Avengers that we would use were already there waiting for us in a hangar next to that occupied by the helicopters of 705. The ship's flight, commanded by Lieutenant

Commander Gerry Bricker, late of 705 staff, with the other two pilots, Johnny Plant and Griff Griffiths, were working up the helicopters together. Johnny and Griff were dual qualified to back Dennis and me up as fixed-wing pilots. Our observers were also at Lee, Lieutenants John Williams and Derek Field, who was to fly mostly with me, although both could crew helicopters if required. I was immediately impressed by the friendly way the unit gelled together, helped to a great extent by Gerry's wife, Penny.

Gerry and Penny lived just outside the base and kept almost open house for us. I managed to rent a small Bungalow at Stubbington for the few months remaining before embarkation and Johnny Plant had a rented place not too far away. In no time at all, we bonded into a very happy little flight with a good social side while we worked up for the task ahead. Being now closely associated with helicopters I was able to see what interesting, versatile beasts they were. Although I thoroughly enjoyed flying the Avenger, as I had the Gannet, I was soon resolved to fly helicopters at the earliest opportunity. I could see that the new roles developing for rotary-winged aircraft indicated that, together with fighter squadrons, the helicopter would form the two main components of the Fleet Air Arm in a year or so. I was also becoming very aware that I was at my happiest in small units working on specific but varied tasks, and a rotary-wing pilot seemed to fit the bill admirably; the whole anti-submarine world was in the throes of great change.

We now knew that we would be embarking in *Warrior* in the New Year and going to operate in the Pacific for at least nine months. Telegraphist Green joined Derek and me and together we practised the flying tasks that would be expected of us at Christmas Island on Operation Grapple, as it was known.

By now, I was enjoying flying the 'Turkey'. It was a steady, dependable ride and to date had given good reliable service; it certainly lived up to its reputation as a really rugged aircraft. Only on one thing was I at a distinct variance with my crew. It was a very cold winter and often, in the draughty Avenger, Derek or

Green would ask if we could have the aircraft heater turned on. The heater was a weird contraption in the Avenger, and it sounded decidedly dangerous. It appeared that it consisted of an electrically heated plate onto which high octane, from the fuel tanks, was dripped and subsequently ignited. The resulting fire produced heat that was ducted through to the cockpits. As there was no way I was going to allow petrol to be ignited in my aircraft, other than in the engine cylinders and also, as I had the relevant controls in my cockpit, we all had to shiver safely until we landed and got back into the fug of the crew-room.

As the leaving date drew closer, we were practising ADDLs every day. The good residents of Lee-on-Solent must have been demented listening to the roar of Cyclone engines as we skated round the circuit at 400 feet, eyes fixed on the batsman at the end of the runway, thumping down as he 'chopped' his flags and then roaring off again to repeat the whole process. Of course fate was, as ever, looking over my shoulder and biding her time in the wings. By Christmas we were about ready, and after the festive break we made our first acquaintance with HMS *Warrior* in the Channel on 6 January 1957, when we carried out, for me at any rate, my first batted landings on a straight deck. I found that occasionally I had a problem with the final stage of the deck landing. I tended to leave the 'flare', essential to placing the hook in the wires, too late. This meant that the aircraft landed on its main wheels first. The soft oleos caused the aircraft to bounce, preventing the hook from connecting with the wires. It needed a really positive pull back on the control column to sit the Avenger down on three wheels. A pilot in this position had no forward vision at all except the huge blue nacelle of the engine and I think that subconsciously, I felt a lack of control. The batsman briefed me on what he could see was wrong and with more practice I overcame the problem, but I never enjoyed those last few seconds when I could see nothing ahead and the aircraft was in a stalled state but not yet in contact with the deck.

We stayed on board until the 10th when we returned to Lee-on-Solent to continue ashore until 2 February. With our final farewells completed, we embarked in *Warrior* and sailed towards the Atlantic for the crossing to our next objective; the Panama Canal.

As we passed Ushant, at the entrance to the Atlantic itself, we were struck by wind and seas of hurricane force; within a few hours the ship was battering through mountainous seas that broke over the bridge, 60 feet above the surface of the sea. The winds ripped off one of the radio masts above the bridge and, in the hangar deck below, the aircraft were tugging and hopping about like frightened horses, lashed down with their restraining wires. A particularly big wave smashed into the bow at flight deck level, crushing the paint store in the bow. In doing so it split several tins of paint and forced the contents through the access hatch causing a multi coloured psychedelic pattern around the door. I think that some thirty feet of the upper bow was hammered in.

We aircrew at the stern were relatively comfortable. As latecomers to the carrier, our cabins had been allocated in the depths of the ship four or five decks down. The more salubrious, upper deck cabins had been taken by the ship's officers, which I thought quite understandable. Suddenly, there was a flurry of activity. We were ousted from our cabins and moved up to the upper cabins. We soon discovered why. With the violent movements of the ship, it was practically impossible to stay in your bunk and, on the higher decks, the motion was very much worse. The sensation, lying in one's bunk, was rather like that of being in a tin trunk that was being pulled down a flight of stairs, with a pronounced roll as well. The ship's watch keeping officers reasoning was that they needed their rest whilst, for the moment, we were just passengers. Again, a perfectly reasonable argument I thought, as I grimly braced myself in anticipation of the next attempt to hurl me out of my bunk. They had to man the ship watch on, watch off; all we had to do was continuously check the lashings on the aircraft in the hangar deck as they leapt about like nervous animals.

I did feel sorry though, for a fairly large contingent of RAF and Army ranks. They had elected to come on the sea trip instead of the usual transport flight out to Christmas Island. Wracked with seasickness, they rolled about helplessly, immersed in their misery and the seas that washed from the weather decks, along the passageways where their hammocks were slung. Most of them felt they were dying; the others thought they were already dead; I think all of them prayed for a happy release. It was a violent start to the voyage.

After three turbulent days the weather settled, the seas turned blue and the sun came out. We ploughed on towards the Caribbean and on to the Panama Canal. Within twenty-four hours everyone, including our unfortunate guests, was in a jaunty mood. The ship had suffered badly in the hurricane and was said to be pumping out the 400 tons of water a day that was entering through the damaged bow. During this quiet passage, the weather steadily improved until it was continuously the sparkling sun and blue skies with star filled nights so beloved by the holidaymaker.

Unfortunately the health of the ship's padre was now causing some concern. He had become unwell shortly after sailing, as did many people, but his condition had persisted and had now deteriorated; it was thought that he had a kidney stone. A decision was made to fly him off to Kingston, Jamaica, about 300 miles away, to obtain treatment in the hospital there. An Avenger was brought up to the flight deck and the padre and the shipwright, who had business ashore, prepared to board. I was already strapped in and briefed for a catapult launch. Why the catapult? Only Flyco, which was the department on the ship in charge of flying operations, and the padre's boss, knew the answer to that question. Wrapped in blankets and looking decidedly ill, our spiritual guidance officer was carefully stowed in the rearmost cockpit; a claustrophobic tunnel in the rear fuselage, entered through a little door, and normally occupied by Telegraphist Green. The shipwright, somewhat tight-lipped and noticeably pale, reluctantly clambered into the observer's position. He had spent his naval life in the depths of a ship, responsible for the upkeep of its structural safety; I gathered that this was to be his first flight and obviously, if he ever got back alive and had a choice, it would certainly be his last.

I started up the engine and trundled up to the catapult and was soon hurled, with that almighty, irresistible force, into the air. All the way to Palisadoes airfield, there was a tangible, nervous silence from my apprehensive passengers. As I switched off the engine and the hospital attendants unloaded the padre and loaded him into an ambulance. He looked considerably chirpier, far more like his old self. I put this down to his relief at having landed safely, and on the right island; a relief I shared wholeheartedly. It later transpired that the considerable jolt of the catapult had caused him to pass the offending stone, and he was now a lot happier. Even so, it was considered unwise for him to continue the voyage and he recovered in Jamaica, before returning to the UK. I reflected that, despite not having pursued a career in medicine, I had in my small way, contributed to the padre's cure or perhaps the ship's surgeon knew a thing or two about the healing properties of a catapult. Now alone, I flew back to the ship, landing successfully, we all rolled on to Panama, only stopping briefly at Kingston to pick up stores and the shipwright, very obviously grateful that he had not been required to fly back.

Within a few days we entered the eastern end of the Panama Canal for the complicated crossing of the isthmus. Famous for its many locks, the Panama Canal presented quite a problem to *Warrior*. Even with her straight deck she just managed to squeeze through the locks. At times terrible scraping sounds were heard and there was little doubt that she would definitely need some paint slapped on when we reached our destination. It took most of a long day to pass through the canal, continually stopping in the locks as water levels were adjusted.

When we were about halfway, a small scruffy looking civilian appeared in the wardroom wishing to sell 'shrunken heads' as souvenirs, assuring all and sundry that they were human. We all stared, bemused, at the gruesome looking heads until I think it was the doctor declared that they were, in fact, monkey heads. Protesting loudly that his goods were genuine and that we had wasted his valuable time, the repulsive little chap was invited to leave and disappeared to tempt some other customer. The incident did however stay in my memory and I soon had cause to think of our unpleasant little visitor and his revolting trophies.

After reaching the Pacific, the ship once more had to fly off a casualty; an injured rating. He was loaded into an Avenger and with John Cooper as my observer; I flew back to Bogota to land the rating for treatment in the hospital there. While returning to the ship, we had to fly over dense jungle; rugged, hilly and sparsely inhabited country for about an hour. When I saw thin columns of smoke coming up from the occasional habitation amongst the trees, I thought idly about the shrunken heads, and checked all the aircraft instruments very carefully. The Wright Cyclone roared on and the oil pressure stayed constant to reassure me that we were not likely to end up with our heads hanging on someone's bedpost. I was happy to see the grey hulk of *Warrior*, with the wash streaming out behind her, as she got up to speed in order to land me on as I made my approach from the fast fading shores of South America.

In glorious Pacific weather we pushed on past the Galapagos Islands towards Christmas Island, with several days sailing ahead to reach that distant speck in this vast ocean.

A day or so away from the island, I was again launched with my normal crew for Christmas Island. The mission was to pick up a naval liaison officer from the island and return with him to *Warrior*. The trip was uneventful although it was fascinating to land at the airfield to see something of what was going on. It appeared to be a barren place, hacked out of the coral and sandstone surrounded by coconut palms, with prefabricated buildings at one end of a runway that was long enough to accommodate a large bomber. After landing on the dusty field, I was instructed by air traffic control to taxi over and park by the Canberra bombers quietly gleaming a similar blue to my own craft but looking far more elegant.

Our hosts were the RAF Canberra squadron based on the island for reconnaissance duties and sample collection. They were to be our hosts on all of the occasions that we visited or stayed on the base. They were a friendly bunch, highly amused at our arrival. They couldn't believe that anything as old, or looking like our 'Turkey', could possibly fly. The greater part of their flying was at very high altitudes and they were quick to clamour for any trips we might do, if and when we carried out general flying on the island. They were not so enthusiastic about joining us for deck landing practice.

Lieutenant Commander Thatcher duly arrived at the squadron offices, after declaring that he had very little experience of flying. I briefed him about various safety drills necessary in any emergency, and he enthusiastically climbed into Telegraphist Green's cockpit in the tunnel at the rear of the aircraft. We said our grateful farewells and taxied out to take-off, anxiously watched by Green and our incredulous new friends. Once airborne, I carried out a low pass just to prove our airworthiness to the RAF and returned to *Warrior*, which still had some way to go before she reached Christmas Island.

The flight back was as uneventful as the one to Christmas Island. That is, until I rejoined to land. My approach was fine, with a happy batsman signalling a normal landing. As I came over the round down, he gave me the signal to throttle back and land. I obeyed, but a brief lapse in concentration let me thump down on the deck with the cursed tail wheel still well up in the air. The main wheels, with their soft oleos, compressed and then threw the Avenger back into the air. For a few short seconds that seemed like a lifetime, I was not moving. Fifty feet up in the air, but stationary, attached to HMS *Warrior* like a fly in a spider's web, I forlornly gazed down at the startled, open-mouthed faces looking up at me from Flyco on the bridge. It quickly dawned on me that I had caught the carrier with my hook and now there was nowhere else to go but down. With a teeth jarring crash, the plane fell back on the deck, bursting both tyres and leaving two dents in the deck that stayed with *Warrior* forever. Thankfully, the famous sturdiness of the Avenger absorbed all the injury and she stood there ticking and looking wounded with a distinct droop in the engine, as I clambered sheepishly out of the cockpit. Deeply ashamed, I walked down the wing and jumped down to the deck, to meet the unfortunate Lieutenant Commander Thatcher ducking out of the rear door. Before I could apologise, he thanked me for 'a very nice flight'. A real gentleman, I thought, but what sort of pilots had he flown with previously?

I had no one to blame but myself. The CO and Commander (Air) were very cool but kind about it, reasoning that because of the time factor, we had very little opportunity for deck landing practice. I confess, I would never have thought of that as an excuse, but there was an element of truth in it. My instructors at Eglinton, who had wryly watched my main wheel landings would not have been so tolerant. I sadly went down to my cabin to write up my A25, an accident report, notorious in naval aviation circles, and a full, written explanation was required of every pilot following an accident where an aircraft was damaged. At least I had not lost or injured anyone; only the Avenger and *Warrior* were badly dented, together with my ego. My overconfident blasé landing had been 'pilot error' without a doubt and at only one attempt, I had wrecked half of the fixed-wing component of *Warrior*'s ship's flight, and we hadn't reached the island yet.

Shortly after reaching the island, we discovered that the ship had to go to Honolulu for stores and some repairs. A replacement Avenger had been found in the USA and would be waiting, crated, in Pearl Harbor. Within a few days we were entering Pearl Harbor, the American naval base whose attack by the Japanese, had triggered the American entry to the Second World War in 1941. We moored alongside, welcomed by a USN silver band playing Souza, and Hawaiian girls with plastic flower leis and plastic hula skirts, dancing on the dockside. There was just a week or so to complete repairs and provision. During that time with the others, I managed to get ashore and visit the famous beach and the town. It was a disappointment to me, everything seemed very 'Hollywood movie set' and rather artificial. What interested me most was to see the giant crate containing the replacement Avenger swing on board. I'm sure that Hawaii and its adjacent islands are very beautiful but we did not have the time to explore.

The ship sailed back to Christmas Island to prepare for the first drop of a test bomb. While the ground crew feverishly assembled the new Avenger in the hangar deck we practised deck landings and general flying and the helicopter crews rehearsed the strange routines that would be required of them once down at the target island. This involved, amongst other things, dressing up in bulky suits and wearing a form of gas mask while flying. It was extremely cumbersome and was, I think, discarded before the event. The risk of contamination was considered far less than that of controlling a helicopter, wearing a mask and dressed in the suits. I was intrigued to see the newly built Avenger, un-crated in the hangar, being reconstructed by the ground crew. It was still in its American colours; in addition to the stars instead of roundels it had gaily painted red and white stripes horizontally painted on its rudder. Apparently its previous owners had been the US Coastguard at a place called El Centro. Whilst I was quite happy to fly under false colours, the powers that be insisted that the new aircraft be painted in the standard naval strip.

As we once again approached Christmas Island, the two remaining Avengers were disembarked to keep in flying practice ashore. While staying with our friendly Canberra squadron, who were also preparing for the big day, I carried out a lot of general flying around the island and plenty of dummy deck landings were practised on the main runway. Sometimes the Canberra boys begged a lift and were always delighted to skate around the island at low level, a thing they were never able to do in their Canberras. The only protesters were the thousands of sea birds nesting on the uninhabited side of the island and, for my own safety, I kept well clear by flying over the coral reef that lay half a mile offshore. The birds very soon became used to the disturbance.

Christmas Island is shaped like a lobster with its claws embracing the circular lagoon opening to the sea at the north-western end. The tail stretches towards the south-east some thirty-five miles. It is about twenty-five miles wide at the 'head and claws' end, where the main camp and airfield were situated. The harbour as such, was at a jetty, extending out from a village called Port London, situated at the tip of the northern claw. A few resident islanders remained in the village, scratching a living from the coconut and copra plantations on the island; many had accepted the opportunity to evacuate to another island until the tests were over. The remaining islanders kept very much to themselves and they were friendly enough; there was a certain amount of interaction as the ship's boats used the jetty extensively. The post office was particularly popular with its own stamps and a few native artefacts available. By far the largest population on the island were the land crabs; there were millions of them, living quietly by day in the shady scrub around the palms, but scavenging in their hordes as soon as the sudden, windless twilight fell. They gave off an odd musty smell that was almost overpoweringly unpleasant. At night they covered the roads, or rather tracks, and adopted threatening postures in the vehicle headlights. They paid the penalty for their boldness with horrid crunching sounds and an even more pungent smell. Their more fortunate comrades then, with apparent relish, eagerly consumed their remains. I am quite sure that no one serving out there has ever forgotten the land crabs, especially the poor man who awoke on his low camp bed one morning, to find it unusually dark. It was a land crab, sitting on his face, with its mouth parts flickering to and fro an inch from his eyes as if contemplating a feast. His frantic screams were heard all over the camp.

The main camp and airfield were a little further on from Port London and then the rest of the 'lobster's body' was largely left as the arid dunes, the scrubby domain of the thousands of seabirds. This provided great 'expedition' and 'banyan' country, easily accessible by the naval Land-Rover, whenever it was available for recreational purposes.

In early April 1957, the *Warrior* sailed from Christmas to Malden Island, the target island. Malden was a very different place from the main base. Hundreds of miles from anywhere, it was an uninhabited lump, almost barren with a scrubby landscape. It was now temporarily inhabited by scores of scientists and technicians, setting up their particular recording equipment in order to be ready for the detonation of the first of the atomic bombs.

Without a runway or landing ground of any sort on Malden, the helicopters now came into their own and were constantly in the air. Dennis and I were briefed on the role we fixed-wing pilots would play on the day of the drop. The choppers were to evacuate the scientific team from the island to the carrier prior to the explosion. After the event, and a suitable safety delay, they would be returned by helicopter to collect their 'samples'. As we had to withdraw the ship to twenty-six miles or so from Malden for safety reasons, this would take some time, during which an Avenger would be ranged on the catapult to be loaded with material collected by the scientists and brought back from the island by the helicopters for onward routing to the UK via Christmas Island. The material was to be accompanied by a scientist, certainly as far as the base island, so Telegraphist Green would have to yield up his seat in the Avenger once again.

While these preparations were going on, reports were coming in of a possible intrusion by protesters, sailing vessels into the danger area. It had been claimed that they intended to disrupt the operation and everyone was very aware of the threat. In addition, with such a large area of the sea declared prohibited to shipping, it was remotely possible that some mariner ignorant of the ban could stray into danger, despite the aerial patrols by Shackleton aircraft.

Just before 'D' day, an RAF aircraft in the area reported a sail, probably a small boat, close to Malden. With this alarm, *Warrior* sprang into action. The tannoy broadcast that we were going to 'flying stations' and that an Avenger would be launched forthwith. I was briefed to fly the aircraft with Derek and Telegraphist Green in the back. Suddenly bundles of warning leaflets appeared and were stuffed in the back with Green. We were instructed to scatter these over any unofficial craft in the area. That should scare them off.

As there was a steeply shelving beach surrounding the island, *Warrior* steamed past close to shore, at speed, to allow me a normal unassisted take-off. By now the word had spread and the beach was packed with spectators anxious to enjoy the unexpected diversion to their day; an aircraft carrier at speed, passing only 500 yards away and launching aircraft. It was all a very dramatic prelude to the test.

In the Avenger, with full power, I trundled down the deck and lifted off the bow. As I did so, the motor began to fail; the engine revs falling away slowly. I did not want to ditch ahead of the ship and risk being overrun by it so I used what power I had to turn away towards the island, vainly hoping that I would find some flattish place to put down. It was, with hindsight, thankfully, not to be, as Malden doesn't have any flattish places and I was full of highly combustible fuel. Sinking down towards the surf, I raised the wheels and flaps so that there was no obstruction hanging down under the aircraft and warned the crew and the ship that we were going to get wet. Later as I filled my report, I was surprised at what checks I had made, of control positions and instrument readings in the minute so that remained as we gently sank down into the water.

I braced myself for what the survival manuals described as the 'double thump' that a ditching aircraft is expected to make on contact with the water. I believe I may have indulged in some very bad language as we went down. By sheer good luck, I must have entered the water on the top of one of the huge rollers that continuously thundered in to break on the shore at Malden. I don't think even a cupful of water splashed onto my windscreen and the aircraft floated beautifully. As I undid my harness, I looked to the right, preparing to vacate the cockpit; I was amazed to see an absolutely dry Derek Field, standing on the wing, casually inflating his personal dinghy. He placed the dinghy carefully on the dry wing, sat in it and nonchalantly pushed off; it was only then that the rough seas soaked him. By the time I stood in the same place with my dinghy, the poor old 'Turkey' was beginning to settle by the nose. I noted that Green's door was open and that leaflets were floating out in all directions, but there was no sign of Green. As I paddled across the wing, towards his door, to assist, he ducked out, without his dinghy, and bleeding slightly from a head wound. Aware of the island's notorious reputation for sharks, I pulled him into my dinghy and we floated around, precariously sharing my one-man accommodation, to await the helicopter, even now coming to our rescue. As Green was bleeding I sent him up first and then Derek and the laden Whirlwind took them back to the ship. I had a little time left to see the Avenger slip below the surface. Then, to my horror I saw, through the clear depths a dark shape surging towards my flimsy dinghy. I vigorously pulled open the pack of shark repellent stitched to my life saving waistcoat and was immediately covered in a foul tasting black powder. The shark turned out to be the Avenger's wing mounted, blue radar pod that had detached from the sinking aircraft and shot quickly to the surface, where it bobbed alongside my dinghy for a while. Relieved, I saw the rescue helicopter coming back for me and, in no time at all, I arrived back on board dyed black and soaking wet. The 'Turkey' had had the last laugh, and I had another A25 to write.

Immediately, the shocked scientists viewing my mishap had convened an emergency union meeting and unanimously passed a resolution declaring that there was no way that one of their members would ever put a foot in an Avenger. We 'maniacs' would have to transport the samples to Christmas Island by ourselves. Green went to the sickbay to be patched up, later to be told he had his cockpit back for the Christmas Island run. Derek went below to change his wet clothes leaving me to explain what had occurred to the CO, Commander (Air) and an interested flight engineer officer, before going below to change and fill out yet another A25. I was well aware of the maxim that a junior officer must keep his name appearing before his senior officers in order to be 'known', but this was ridiculous and I worried in case their Lordships were even now 'marking my card'.

At least this accident was not my fault; it was thought that the propeller pitch control unit had failed at take-off. Further speculation had decided that it was a giant Manta ray that had been the 'sail'. Apparently they cruise on the surface with one wing hoisted above the surface in order to catch the wind, their under belly is white and the triangular fin could look very like a sail from the air; so the protesters were innocent of trespass and, to my knowledge, never infringed our prohibited area. I reflected on how lucky we had all been to escape so lightly from the accident. But now I had reduced the Avenger fleet down to one, with another under construction. Not one bomb had yet been dropped.

It was fortuitous that El Centro, the new aircraft picked up from Pearl Harbor and called after the name on the fuselage, had now been assembled and was ready for her test flight. As I had dented the other Avenger beyond repair, we only had the spare left, and it was only right that I should test fly the replacement. On 8 May, a week after ditching, I climbed away from *Warrior* to check out the new bird, still painted in her bright US markings. She handled every bit as well as had the bent version, now used as spares in the hangar below the flight deck. There was a bit of a fright when all the fuel tank warning indicators blinked on, indicating failure after about fifty minutes' flying. However the engine continued to roar away quite happily, so fuel was getting through, but I called the ship about the problem and they suggested that I land immediately. After landing without mishap, it was, as expected, discovered to be an electrical glitch. By 11 May, we were back at Malden for the first 'drop' with two serviceable Avengers.

The first bomb test, as anticipated, went well; the ship's crew sat on the deck twenty-six miles away and watched the spectacle in awe. As the bomber made its run to the target, everyone was ordered to face away from the island so that eyes would not be damaged by the flash of the detonation. We sat on the flight deck with our backs to the burst. A minute or so later the atom bomb exploded with surprisingly little noise. After a minute we were swept by a very warm blast that I can only liken to a hot oven door being opened with a fan driving the air into the kitchen. Temperatures returned to normal and we were then, after a minute or two, allowed to stand and turn round to see the results of our combined efforts. We turned and took our first look at the incredibly awesome sight over Malden Island. A column of dazzling white smoke, dust and steam was shooting up towards the heavens; the island was completely obscured, dominated by a huge cloud of orange dust. The rapidly rising column was a dazzling white; wreathed with apricot tones that was perhaps more dust, and the lower levels were suffused with blossoming fire. As it boiled, flared and writhed upwards it developed the famous 'mushroom' top. Everything seemed insignificant to the cloud, and we could look at nothing else. The photograph shows the enormous effect seen from twenty-six miles. There was little or no noise other than a slight rumble and the sight stunned most of those on deck into silence. It was to me, one of the most beautiful sights I had ever seen and I wondered at how man's deadliest weapon could look so lovely.

After a while the men, still gazing at the huge cloud, began to murmur quietly amongst themselves; there was no jubilation or cheering, the spectacle had been too mind-blowingly spectacular for that. Soon the blare of the tannoy ordered them back to duty. *Warrior*'s day had just begun and there was much to do. The fixed-wing aircrew vanished below to change into their flying gear, the helicopter crews, already in flying dress, went for a final briefing, while the ground crew ranged the Whirlwind helicopters and an Avenger. The Avenger was pushed forward from the lift to take its place on the catapult. The helicopters, now manned by their crews, stayed aft waiting for the signal to embark the scientists and return them to the haze of dust that was the target island. Soon crowds began to gather round the choppers and the crews started them up. With the teams of scientists safely on board, they lifted off and clattered away towards Malden. Derek and I, together with Green, made our way to the bow to man our Avenger, now sitting on the catapult at the bow. The helicopters estimated that it would take forty to fifty minutes to complete their tasks and return to the ship, so there was no particular hurry for us. We waited by our aircraft, softly discussing what we had seen; the deck crew too were unusually quiet. We finally manned the Avenger and settled into our respective cockpits to wait for the returning choppers. Sitting strapped into a hot cockpit in the full sun was not my idea of fun, and I stared ahead at the glassy, empty sea waiting to make my small contribution to history. I wondered about what they would find on the devastated island, still covered in a sandy haze, twenty-six miles away.

We were soon advised that the choppers were returning, but just before we started our engine, the deck crew around us all rushed off to peer down over the side of the ship. Intrigued, I called one over and asked him what was so interesting in the water. 'There's a bloody great shark, Sir, going along with us. Must be all of twenty-five feet.' After the earlier ditching it was not the most reassuring thing I had heard all day. I decided I would not share my news with my long-suffering crew. The helicopters landed back on board, sample boxes and reels of film were thrust in upon the unfortunate Green and with engine bellowing at full throttle, the catapult, as usual, flung us safely into the air. We were off on the first 400 mile leg to Christmas Island, to link up with RAF Canberras and finally Vulcans who would have the samples back in the UK within twenty-four hours.

Our flight was uneventful; we picked up the fresh water distillation plant, belching out a column of black at about fifty miles from the still invisible island. The rusty old machine, like a big Victorian traction engine had been resurrected after lying unused since the Crimean War. It was vital for the fresh water supply on the base, but it was hardly spring water and Derek, for one, preferred to clean his teeth with whisky. It made an excellent homing beacon for me. Christmas Island kindly sent a Shackleton out to meet us and escort us for the last 100 miles or so out from Christmas. Escorted by the big bomber, we were gently led into the airfield after more than two hours' of flight over an empty ocean.

After a few days spent with the Canberra squadron or in the Officers' Mess on Christmas Island, while *Warrior* was returning to base, we waited for orders. If required, we would fly out to land on and rejoin the ship. Usually, we stayed on the island for general flying practice and rejoined her as she was outward bound again for Malden.

Mess life with the Army was an interesting affair. The whole base was a tented one, except for the prefabricated building erected as a social centre and used by the NAAFI. Two ladies, the only ones on the base, who cheerfully staffed it, kept all and sundry well supplied with anything from razor blades to sticky buns. The Mess tent provided good food, although if the Michelin guide had visited, I don't think any stars would have been forthcoming. Surrounding the main tent were the rows of tents in which we slept on flimsy camp beds. Sleep for us strangers, unused to life ashore, tended to be 'fitful'. At night there was always the continual rustle of foraging land crabs to contend with as they roamed around, and occasionally in, the tents. It was one of the stillest places on the planet that I have ever been to, with absolutely no movement of air on some occasions. One would see fellow officers smoking outside their tents and having to walk away from exhaled smoke as it hung in the still air. Of course it did eventually disperse but only very slowly. Other interests were the submerged vehicles recovered by the army engineers. Jeeps and other equipment had been dumped at the edge of the reef at the end of the war by the departing US forces. When they arrived on the island, the innovative engineers had quickly recovered some and restored them to use, painting them some very gaudy colours to show they were now in private hands.

By the end of May we were back at Malden for the second drop on 31 May. It was a routine affair until we were approaching Christmas Island and the Shackleton once again met us. As he closed, he nonchalantly asked me if I knew I was on fire. He added that the Avenger was trailing white smoke from the engine. Needless to say, this set the adrenalin flowing, and loosening my harness; I opened the hood and leant out into the slipstream to see if I could spot the source of the fire. My face was immediately covered with warm oil. Ducking back into the cockpit, I realized there was little I could do but press on to Christmas Island with the Shackleton formating on me like a concerned mother hen. On landing, it was found that a cylinder head gasket had blown and leaked fourteen of my twenty-one gallons of oil. One side of the aircraft was covered with shiny oil, with me included. I was relieved to think we did not have another 100 miles to go. With the samples on board, another 'ditching' would have set the whole test back. Two days later I flew back to the ship. Once back on board, the Commander (Air) wanted to see me. He had been invited by the Admiralty to offer me an extension of service to twelve years. I had great pleasure in accepting their kind offer.

On 20 June the final drop was made and I flew to Christmas Island with the samples; a routine run without incident. I returned to the ship on the 22nd. That, as far as we were concerned, was the end of the task, and my Avenger days were over. On reading my ageing log book as I wrote these words, I have come to realize that I did the larger part of the fixed-wing flying on Operation Grapple; Dennis must have kept a very low profile. In my enthusiasm as a young flyer, I had never noticed that he was not available to share the flying duties.

The last remaining days on Christmas Island were spent relaxing. About half a dozen of the aircrew had been told of lobsters, in their hundreds, that could be easily caught by hand on the reef at night, so we decided to take an all night trip on one of the last nights ashore. We borrowed the Land-Rover and drove down to the reef. We waited for night to fall and then lit up the Tilly lamps. Shining them over the barely covered reef revealed what were in fact giant, clawless crayfish, their eyes glinting red in the lamp light; as promised, in their hundreds. Wearing stout leather gloves, we slaved away all night managing to catch over 400. Once on board, they needed freezing but this problem was easy to solve. In the forward part of the hangar, a large refrigerated room had been built before we left UK. The reason for its construction was never sought, or given, but it had contained scientific material relating to the tests, that needed refrigeration. Now, it was both redundant and empty. We handed our precious catch over to the catering officer who stocked the room with our crayfish. We were anticipating some wonderful meals in the wardroom, on the way home. This, however, was not the end of the voyage, there was still a lot of sailing to be done, and it was rumoured that fascinating times lay ahead.

Chapter 11

One Elderly Aircraft Carrier for Sale

The rumours quickly became fact. We were to return home by way of South America and, on the way, try to sell HMS *Warrior*. This would be the cream on the cake after Operation Grapple. Few of HM aircraft carriers had the opportunity to visit this part of the world in post war days. We said our farewells to those who were staying behind to tidy up. I was surprised that those Army and RAF personnel, who had suffered such an uncomfortable trip out, were clamouring to return with us, accepting the considerable delay in getting home. Sadly their requests were denied and we sailed away from Christmas Island, although not directly for South America.

The *Warrior* churned away southwards as if unsure where the Americas lay. It transpired that we were to call on one or two islands south of Malden, amongst them Penryhn, Raratonga, now a holiday resort island, and Pitcairn, famous as the home of the descendants of the *Bounty* mutineers.

Penryn was a small, sparsely inhabited island, where a small band of American radio operators and, I think, meteorologists were based. I was not lucky enough to go ashore with the helicopters. I was intrigued however, to hear of the fuselage and other wreckage of a Second World War Liberator or similar type, mouldering away in the undergrowth behind the village. I wondered how it arrived at its final resting place and the circumstances. To whom did it belong; did they know it was there and what happened to the crew? After a very brief stop, we were soon under way for Raratonga.

Raratonga, in the Cook Island group was a really beautiful tropical island with a fairly large Polynesian population, well administered by New Zealand. It was truly idyllic and in order to preserve the culture of the native inhabitants, the New Zealand Government had imposed strict limitations on any new settlement. There were no missionaries as their conversion practices had destroyed much of the Polynesian culture that was passed down the generations by word of mouth. Just before we arrived, the administration had ordered two dentists off the island. They had been stranded when their yacht ran aground on the reef. Soon, surviving on Raratonga worked its magic and they wanted to stay. The administration decided that, even a dentist had nothing to offer the island that would improve the Maori way of life and they were ordered off. I thought that their policies were extremely practical and to the people's advantage. Nowadays I see it is firmly established as an international holiday resort and I wonder just how many of those lofty principles remain. We stayed a few days there and were royally entertained by the chief and his family. The Maoris were a happy people, always smiling, friendly and relaxed; one was easily led to forget their extremely warlike nature. As had Captain Cook, so did we.

In our innocence, or in a fit of madness, the ship, (no one person would admit responsibility later), challenged the island rugby club to a match with the, up to that date, non-existent ship's team. As mad as the rest, I volunteered for hooker, my position in my schooldays. We were all confident that even without practice and a team newly formed at short notice, we would give a very good account of ourselves. As military men, we should have remembered that the same overconfidence and lack of planning has caused most of history's classic military disasters. The widely assorted and experienced or otherwise ship's talent arrived at the island's pitch wearing an assortment of rugby kit that would have brought tears to a selector's eyes.

The whole island turned out to watch. Good-natured but, no doubt, well aware of the outcome, they settled noisily under some shady palms and happily waited for the game to start. It was extremely hot, and the pitch appeared to be made of ground coral and cement with a few sorry looking blades of grass struggling to survive the hostile environment. The only qualification for the label 'pitch' was the correct measurements and two sets of rather dilapidated posts at either end.

As we kicked the ball about before the kick-off, small boys ran all over the pitch helping us retrieve the balls. As a huge smile is the everyday expression of these people, it was difficult to guess whether they were genuinely glad to see us, or just anticipating the slaughter that was to come. We quickly noticed that these small boys aged 6 or so, could punt a ball nearly the length of the pitch, in bare feet. It slowly began to dawn on us that we had definitely 'bitten off more than we could chew'. And so it turned out. Most of their players, each one about 16 stone, in an immaculate kit but bare footed, could comfortably cover 100 yards in 11 seconds, whilst conserving their energy so that they could keep up to speed for the whole match. To be tackled was like being knocked down by a bus and dragged along a newly gritted road. As you lay there, gasping through tortured lungs, and trying to work out which bones remained unbroken, a couple of beaming, un-winded Maoris would cheerfully pick you up and carry you back to the fray.

I now forget the final score, but I don't think we scored at all. On the rare occasions that any one of us got the ball, it resulted in a pitifully desperate attempt, by the unfortunate holder, to get rid of it before he ended up buried in some foreign field by at least 16 stone of charging Maori with a beaming grin. My fondest memory is of the delicious oranges, served at half time; my worst, is having to take part in the second half when the whistle sounded.

However, the islanders saw the game as a great success, and *Warrior* supporters and survivors were invited to the big feast afterwards. The food, whole pigs and several chickens, wrapped in banana leaves, had been cooking in a huge pit since early morning. It was layered with hot charcoal and then covered with earth, the food, to be exhumed just before the feast. As we, exhausted, battered and bleeding ambassadors of good will, enjoyed their wonderful hospitality, I could not help but wonder at how many early missionaries had suffered a far, far more personal acquaintance with this form of barbeque than I.

Having left Raratonga the ship turned her bow towards South America. We stopped briefly at Pitcairn Island as we passed. Because of the heavy surf that protects the island, landing a boat is dangerous to all but the inhabitants, who have developed techniques to deal with the problem. The helicopters, of course, were immune to such limits, and a courtesy visit was made and the headman brought on board to return the compliment. Having left Pitcairn, we carried on towards Peru, the first of our South American visits. We also had the first, and although we did not know it then, our last, wardroom meal of the delicious crayfish we had spent the night catching at Christmas Island. The CO, Gerry Bricker, told us on this leg of the voyage, that we would all get preferential postings on return to the UK. I immediately stated that I would like a conversion onto helicopters, a goal I had always wanted to achieve.

As we crossed the Pacific there was a small matter to resolve regarding the Avengers, now sitting forlornly down in the hangar, unwanted and unused. They were apparently ours under the old Lease-Lend agreement between the USA and Great Britain, made during the Second World War. The Royal Navy, having no further use for them, was obliged to ask America what they required us to do with them. Their answer was immediate. Ditch them in deep water. With many others, I was aghast at such a waste of perfectly good aircraft that had served us so well. I felt it was akin to disposing of a faithful dog just because it was no longer useful.

The disposal order was carried out with due ceremony, watched by a saddened pilot and a jolly crew. The remaining two aircraft and the wreck were catapulted off the ship and were left bobbing in our wake as we sped on to Callao, the port of Lima, Peru. As we entered the harbour with, as usual, ship's flight manning the bow, I noted some old First World War submarines tied up alongside some equally old frigates. When we were alongside, it was decided that, as a gesture of goodwill, we would open the ship to the public for a day. The Peruvian liaison officer advised that, in the first instance, we should restrict the admission to holders of British citizenship papers. The resulting queue was five deep and stretched for nearly a mile, through the dockyard and away up the street outside. Once on *Warrior*, it was impossible to control the crowds; they managed to get everywhere and seemed to have only a vague idea about what was theirs and what was part of the ship. One individual was stopped as he struggled down a ladder-way from the bridge with the yeoman's 10-inch signalling lamp in his arms.

Four days later we sailed south for Chile. At Valparaiso, the Chilean naval liaison officer boarded us, landing on the deck in a small Bell helicopter. He was a cheerful lieutenant commander wearing 'wings' on his uniform. He was delighted with his duty, as he and a number of Chilean officers were trying to persuade their Admiralty to form a naval air arm in their Service. A few had obtained private flying licences and I believe they had a few small helicopters. I thought he was going to cry when we told him of our recently ditched Avengers.

These were very social visits with a lot of high-ranking officials visiting the ship, and lavish entertainment was both given and received as *Warrior* was marketed. We sailed from Chile for the long haul through the Straits of Magellan to our next ports of call, the Falkland Islands and Argentina. Notorious for bad weather and poor visibility, the Straits were, unusually, almost flat calm with perfect visibility. The bleak mountains sweeping down to the sea were very like parts of Scotland and I was not surprised to hear that descendants of Welsh settlers populated Tierra del Fuego and Patagonia. A day or so after clearing the Straits of Magellan we moored in the bay, off Port Stanley, the

Falkland Islands. A group of islands with very strong bonds with the UK, we were made very welcome. Long coveted by the Argentine, the English settlers are always pleased to see a British military presence. The only incident that springs to mind while at this chilly, far flung outpost will possibly evoke memories in many a harbour watch keeper.

I was the officer of the watch as the last liberty boat brought happy, well lubricated sailors back from Port Stanley. I, together with the regulating staff, could tell they were happy because we could hear the raucous singing long before we could spot the MFV. It was well after midnight. As the boat came in range of the lights, we could see that the happiest matelot of all was an inebriated stoker. The regulating chief warned me to stay well clear as any offence against an officer would inevitably be serious for the man. With the MFV still ten or so yards from the ship, the stoker misjudged the distance and tried to step aboard. Plunging into the icy water, he was quickly hauled back onto the MFV by his exuberant but unsympathetic friends and they all stumbled up the gangway to present themselves on deck and then to hurry down to the warmth below decks. The soaking wet drunk was now stone cold sober and song-less after his freezing bath. Dripping and leaving a trail of cold sea water, he muttered 'G'night Sir', and gave no trouble whatsoever as he followed his giggling mates down the ladder.

The next day, we were off to Port Arenas, the Argentine Naval Base, and then up to Buenos Aires. We were, as usual, well entertained and I was surprised once more at the large numbers of Argentine citizens who maintained their British links and flocked down to the ship to welcome us. We entertained lavishly. The Commodore, in particular, was very active on behalf of our masters who wished to sell *Warrior*. At every South American stop, there had been cocktail parties, often in the wardroom, but more frequently so many guests were invited that we used the now empty hangar deck. We were also entertaining the various parties who would be interested in the purchase of an aircraft carrier. Often we junior officers were 'invited' to act as hosts when large numbers of guests were expected. At one such soiree, I think in Peru or Chile, a strange little man had sought Dennis Grimes and myself out. Rather oddly dressed in a crumpled, red striped, cream flannel suit, he seemed a bit out of place amongst the dress uniforms and evening dress of the other guests, but he was a man with a purpose. He particularly buttonholed Dennis and me as the fixed-wing pilots in the crew. He soon got down to business. He had some Lancaster bombers, now converted to a civilian role, called the Lancastrian. He desperately needed pilots, namely us, to fly them. As we explained, we were somewhat committed and had no multi-engined or handling experience of large aircraft. He dismissed this as a triviality and then said how simple the job was; we only had to make short flights over the Andes. We quickly made our excuses and went off to mingle.

We left Buenos Aires and crossed the vast River Plata to Montevideo, where we repeated the entertaining process. By now, our thoughts were centred more on home than hospitality. We were pleased to hear that the Brazilians had decided to give HMS *Warrior* a home. She was to become Brazilian and in due course be called *Independencia*.

At last we sailed for the UK. To celebrate I suggested to the wardroom catering officer that we should dine on a few more of our Christmas Island crayfish. He looked at me blankly and then sheepishly confessed that the Commodore, on his lavish entertaining around the Americas, had used them all; with great effect, if that was any consolation. Disappointed and furious, I broke the news to the other members of the syndicate who had slaved all night on that distant reef, that our dreams of gourmandizing were dashed. I still think that the polite and proper thing to do would have been to mention to us first the intention to use our crayfish in this manner. The fault lies with the catering officer. I can imagine how delighted he must have been, when we asked him to keep 400 'brownie points' in his freezer.

That was the end of Operation Grapple and I was delighted to meet my wife on the dockside at Portsmouth, and to get my desired next appointment to convert to helicopters with 705 Squadron, whose new commanding officer was to be Gerry Bricker, my present CO in *Warrior*. I joined in November 1957, back once more at Lee-on-Solent, Hampshire.

Chapter 12

The Ups and Downs of a Rotary Wing Pilot

I took my first faltering steps towards helicopter conversion on 28 November 1957. It was a dual flight in a Hiller HT1 with Lieutenant Commander Spreadbury as my instructor. He had just completed his instruction of His Royal Highness Prince Philip in the art of helicopter control. Although I sympathized with his loss of prestige by royal patronage, and reduction to once again having to train lesser mortals, I was delighted to have an instructor with such lofty credentials. Needless to say, he was an excellent instructor and also a very nice person.

The Hiller was a small basic trainer, seemingly built of odd bits and pieces. Two persons could sit side by side in the tiny bubble cockpit. It was a strange sensation, the feeling that you were suspended in a large goldfish bowl with a whirling two bladed fan keeping you in the air. First impressions did not inspire confidence or a feeling of security. Ted Spreadbury's demonstration of an 'autorotation', the safe landing procedure carried out after simulated engine failure, was positively alarming. Trapped in the bubble, without the comfort of the familiar parachute, the helicopter seemed to hurtle towards the ground at a terrifying rate. When a crash seemed inevitable, Ted pulled back the control column inducing a satisfying 'flare' to a hover, followed by a slight bump as the skids touched the ground. I was impressed both by his skill and the fact that in a helicopter, one could carry out a forced landing without power, with little or no forward speed, into a very small area. As there was no other way of escape from the aircraft it provided a one-off chance of surviving engine failure. In a fixed-wing aircraft, this would have entailed a slide, out of control, of several hundred feet, demolishing anything in the path of the aircraft. The other option for the fixed-wing aircrew but not available to rotary-wing crews, was to take to their parachutes and leave the aircraft to its own devices.

The variable pitch of the Hiller's two main rotor blades was controlled by the pilot using the collective lever to transmit his control movements by means of elastic strops disconcertingly similar to those used by car owners who strap things onto the roof of their cars. An American flat twin Franklin engine usually found in small lorries and trucks, powered it. The Hiller was kept in the air by the sheer strength of its pilot's left arm, and of course, the elastic bands.

Having said that, it was great fun to fly. It was very robust and although fairly primitive, compared with the helicopters then in service, it was an excellent introduction to flying rotary winged aircraft.

The techniques required to fly helicopters differ greatly from those needed for fixed-wing aircraft. The conventional aircraft is inherently stable. This means that, with the controls properly trimmed, it will maintain the chosen flight path for some time without any adjustment by the pilot. The helicopter is not so obliging, being inherently unstable. In those days, before the introduction of modern technology, control of the helicopter depended on continual management by the pilot. Every movement by him, of any one control, would require an adjustment to be made to every other. This meant that when flying, the pilot was never able to let go of the controls. The evolution of the helicopter has now left those days long back in the past; today's helicopter is a very sophisticated beast using computer techniques un-visualized in the mid-1950s.

That is how it was in the old days. There was no such thing as a relaxed chopper pilot. It was very like juggling six oranges while riding a unicycle; certainly when one first started.

I soloed in about three hours and then the course followed the pattern of every previous course, with a mixture of solo and dual flights. Of course the exercises were totally different. I could fly over to HMS *Siskin* to the large grassed, unused airfield and practice hovering, spot turns or auto-rotations and where, from a suitable height, you simulated engine failure and tried to arrive at your chosen spot. To make a safe landing, the rapid descent of the helicopter could be used to automatically speed up the freewheeling rotor blades and, having selected a landing spot on the way down, convert the excess rotor blade speed into lift in order to cushion the landing. It was all new and fascinating for me, and the little Hiller handled like a sports car; I enjoyed buzzing around in it for ten hours or so. Eventually Ted Spreadbury decided that I should stop playing with toys and start real work by flying the Sikorsky Whirlwind. This was the main operational helicopter used by the Navy and built under licence at Westlands, Yeovil. The Whirlwinds mostly in service with 705 were the original American version, the Whirlwind HAR1; with the ever reliable Pratt and Whitney 'Wasp' radial engine that also powered the Harvard.

Also available was the Sikorsky Dragonfly. This was the first of the helicopters used in numbers by the Navy, in search and rescue units both ashore and afloat. It had a very limited capacity. It was gradually being replaced by the Whirlwind, a much more capable machine with a capacious cabin situated behind the pilot's cockpit. Approaching the end of my course and having graduated in the Whirlwind, my next appointment came through. It was to be RNAS Eglinton, in the ship's flight, for search and rescue duties. This would mean flying the older Sikorsky Dragonfly helicopter with an Alvis engine. I quickly converted to the Dragonfly at Lee and practised the rescue techniques used at that time. In the restricted confines of the Dragonfly, the crewman and the pilot shared the cockpit; an elongated cabin in fact. The crewman, behind the pilot, conned the pilot over a survivor in order to operate the hoisting winch, positioned at the main door behind the pilot, on the port side. There were two methods employed to uplift a survivor. The first, the cable and strop, consisted of a harness lowered to a fully capable survivor. It was assumed that the survivor would be able to put the strop around his chest, under the arms, and be hoisted by the crewman up to the helicopter to be hauled into the cabin. Of course, sometimes the victim was in no state to struggle with a harness, and the Sproule net was invented to deal with an incapacitated survivor. It was a fairly cumbersome 'fishing net device' that was trawled under a person incapable of helping in his own rescue. I was never very happy with this device as it consisted of some heavy pieces of metal piping around the net. In boisterous conditions with a choppy sea, the net could swing about and this could cause even more injury to the person in the water. Both methods are now consigned to history and modern rescue practice has a crewman who is lowered down to the casualty to assist with the rescue.

The Dragonfly's performance was quite limited and its centre of gravity critical. Poor distribution of weight could cause a sensitive and embarrassing imbalance that could induce a very nose down or tail down attitude when off the ground. At the extreme limits, the imbalance could cause a loss of control. To combat this hazard there was a primitive system of lead weights carried in the aircraft to reposition in order to counteract any imbalance. These weights were disc-shaped 7lb lumps of lead pierced to fit on either two rods in front of the pilot's control console, or attached to two rods aft, jutting out from the fuselage. If flying solo, it was advisable to put two weights aft; if a third person was in the cockpit two more weights were added. It was all somewhat 'hit or miss', rather like ballast in a hot air balloon. It could be disconcerting for instance, if there was a passenger who required winching down to a ship. Outbound, with perhaps three weights on the back pins, the helicopter would be balanced; but having dropped the passenger off, the flight back could be uncomfortably tail down.

Total weight was also critical as I discovered one calm summer's day when providing the rescue helicopter on a survival drill for some German aircrew, based at Eglinton while they took delivery of Gannet aircraft that had been purchased by the German Marine Service. The drill involved the German crews going out in an MFV into the centre of Lough Foyle. They were dressed in the flying gear needed for cold climes. It was a clumsy, thick, rubberized, one-piece suit, immediately nicknamed a 'Goonsuit' by scornful aircrew, but only by those who hadn't ditched in the chilly seas around UK. In addition the Germans were wearing inflated life saving waistcoats. At the briefing I got the feeling that this was their first experience of a helicopter rescue and there was a certain apprehension about the exercise.

When the MFV signalled that it was in position, it was my task to fly out to the area and recover the Germans, one at a time, from the water and deposit them at their squadron dispersal at Eglinton. As I approached the MFV there was a man already in the water, about twenty-five yards from the boat, head bobbing and somewhat anxiously awaiting rescue, watched by his apprehensive colleagues on the boat awaiting their turn. The lough was flat calm and it was impossible to find any helpful wind to assist the hover. I made my approach to the head floating in the glassy sea, and came to the hover as my crewman conned me into a position to lift. He lowered the wire with the strop to the floating man. The German fitted the strop over his head and under his arms and signalled that he was ready to be hoisted the twenty or so feet into the Dragonfly.

I heard my crewman say he was winching up, and then gasp. As the German lifted out of the water my crewman, Harness, could see that the man was all of six feet plus, weighed at least sixteen stone and was, of course, dripping wet. I could feel the wire strumming as he came clear of the water and dangled, instinctively gazing up at his rescuer. At the same time, I discovered, by my view of the shoreline slowly rising up my windscreen, that my helicopter was, in fact, being winched down towards the water and the man just above the water was virtually stationary. With the flat calm, the unfortunate chap was just too heavy for the Dragonfly to lift. I tried to get into forward flight but it was no use, the chopper would have none of it and continued to settle very gently towards the sea. In spite of my efforts the rescue was at an impasse, with me just about holding the hover and the unfortunate German dangling several feet above the sea. I should explain that, for just such an emergency, there was an explosive device in the aircraft that guillotined the wire. Also there was a heavy lead weight above the strop to steady it and stop it blowing around when lowered.

Decisions were required, so I ordered the crewman to cut the wire and let the unfortunate German fall back into the sea. When the wire was cut, the wet German was just below the step of the aircraft, still gazing upwards and no doubt feeling that his ordeal was over. I was perhaps now, only twelve feet or so above the water myself. It was a great relief to be rid of the dripping wet, weighty survivor. I never heard the scream, as he, of course, plummeted back into Lough Foyle with a huge splash, followed by the cut wire and the tensioning weight, which unfortunately struck him between the eyes. He was hauled, dazed, onto the MFV. Released of its load, the helicopter rose like a balloon. Apologizing over the radio for the incident, and the inevitable close of the programme, as we were now wireless, we flew back to base.

Later, in the Mess, the German aviator approached me, sporting a massive bruise on his forehead. Drawing himself up to his full six feet eight inches and glowering aggressively at me, he accused me of cutting the wire deliberately because of his nationality. He said, 'You vood not haf effer don zat to der British pilot'.

I assured him that the reason was for his, and our, safety and asked him: 'What would you have preferred, the lead weight or a three ton helicopter landing on your head?' But now, after his tirade, I didn't feel so bad about the massive bruise he had on his forehead where the lead weight had struck him as he plunged into the water, still looking up at the, now departing helicopter.

Flying with the Search and Rescue flight was a wonderful experience. We were, to a certain extent, our own masters. As long as we were available at short notice while the station was flying and available for any emergency at other times, we were not bothered by anyone. The CO was Lieutenant Commander 'Porky' Meadowcroft, an old and bold chopper pilot on his last commission before retirement. He was a keen photographer and carried his camera on all his flights. He frequently took photos of the large commercial enterprises and anything else of interest in the area and offered them to the provincial newspapers or the developers. His pictures were very popular. The other pilot, Lieutenant Jeremy R. de B Wailes, was apparently of the huntin' and fishin' aristocracy and sometimes, when dressed with the eccentricity demanded of his class, he looked decidedly odd in his favourite hairy, bracken green tweeds with ghillie stockings and deerstalker hat, lumpy brogues, and sporting a hefty blackthorn walking stick. His somewhat languid and seemingly casual approach to flying was highlighted when he insisted on flying his Dragonfly to a position outside the hangar doors. The landing area was bounded by trees and when he turned the aircraft to try and actually fly into the hangar, the tail rotor edged into the foliage and pruned them as effectively as a chainsaw. The tail rotor was smashed, the Dragonfly, luckily for him, thudded onto the ground before the damaged helicopter could whirl round its main rotor. Seemingly unrepentant, Jeremy strode off to complete an A25 accident report. In the report, in the section reserved for 'Reason for Accident', he wrote, 'Sheer bad luck'. This incurred the incandescent wrath of the station commander who interviewed Jeremy at length.

As the remaining pilot I, quite by accident, became the fishing expert in a year that saw record catches of salmon on the Foyle. The salmon were so prolific that local fish and chip shops were selling salmon fillets and chips at a cheaper price than the traditional cod. Being curious about the reported 400 nets in use between Derry and Strabane, I flew over the river to have a look. I was amazed to see how many fishermen offered us salmon, holding them up to us for inspection. I did not know if this happened before but I soon found the reason, the watertight tins of aircrew emergency rations. Designed to provide sustenance to downed aircrew sitting in their dinghy or languishing beside a crashed aircraft, the tins were filled with boiled sweets and jellies. The fishermen valued the tins, as their watertight rubber seals kept their shredded tobacco and cigarette papers dry; also their kids loved the sweets. During subsequent flights, Leading Aircraftsman Harness, my usual crewman, took a wicker waste paper basket attached to a length of cod line. We discovered that the boats fishing at sea were just as keen on the tins and after lowering a waste paper basket containing a few tins of survival rations to them, a mutually satisfactory exchange could take place. We were soon well supplied with fresh fish.

Certain boats even turned like an aircraft carrier into wind so that we could make an approach. We thought that we were a reassuring reminder to them that we were a safety factor, keeping an eye on them as they followed their dangerous profession.

I knew that we had the tacit approval of the captain when he rang to ask me to get him a 6lb salmon as the Flag Officer Flying Training was expected to visit that day. As fate would have it we had a phone call from operations requesting a helicopter to assist in a search around an area in which a suspected terrorist cache had been unearthed. It was way down to the south, well outside our normal area of operations, but off I went. It looked as if the captain was to be disappointed. The search completed, we were on our way home when, to our surprise, we saw a group of men fishing a small river. Up went an arm holding a salmon and down I went, happy to oblige. It turned out to be a fine fish of about 6lbs. I landed on the front lawn of the captain's house, 'minding his bloody tulips' as ordered, and passed the salmon to his steward; job done. I very much doubt if that would be countenanced today. Captain Roberts was always very kind to my wife and I and would ask for me to fly him as his pilot if he required one. Helicopters were welcomed everywhere; it was as if everyone realized what a marvellous invention aviation was developing for the world. Despite the future inventions and discoveries that have been made, I personally think that the versatile, rotary wing aircraft must rank among the best inventions of the twentieth century, and it was my privilege to fly them.

For me, my time at Eglinton was one of my happiest. My wife was with me and we had, for the first time, been allocated a married quarter after a few months' of waiting in rented accommodation. Usually young officers without children had great difficulty in getting a quarter. One accumulated points, based mainly on size of family. Time after time one could reach the top of the list, expecting allocation any day, and be usurped by a newly posted officer with umpteen kids. It was very frustrating, especially when Pat, my wife, who was now pregnant, had to wait in England until the rental became available.

In married quarters it was far easier to respond to search and rescue callouts as we could be airborne and on our way to any incident within minutes.

The months of 1958 passed happily enough, with my son, a first and only child, born in Londonderry in September. For the record, my wife was the only married mother in the maternity ward, but not alone as all the beds were occupied and, as she gleefully reported, the standard farewell to the other departing single mums was, 'See you next year'.

Unfortunately December spoilt our, until then accident free, flying record. At the beginning of December a Gannet, practising rocketing attacks at Minnearney range, shed the outboard sections of both its wings when they broke off as he pulled out of the dive. The pilot with a remarkable piece of flying was able to land the crippled aircraft safely back at Eglinton. The detached wing sections fell in the mud of the lough and lay flat on the surface of the rocket range, quietly filling with water as the tide slowly began to come in. The engineers at Eglinton said that they would like to study the fractured parts; so 'Porky', camera ever at the ready to photograph the unusual, flew out with Harness as his crewman to retrieve them. Burly armourers waded out to the wing and upended it for the strop to be passed around so that it could be lifted for return to Eglinton. 'Porky' was unaware that the wing was now considerably heavier than normal, the compartments now being full of mud and water. With the wing attached to the helicopter by the wire, he attempted to lift it. Straining to break the wing free of the mud was a heavy task for the Dragonfly helicopter. As the hoist was on the port side, he had his controls crossed fully over to the starboard side and the engine at full throttle. Unluckily, Harness, ever since his experience with the Germans, now considered himself to be an expert on wire cutting. Without any reference or warning to the pilot, whose prerogative it should have been, he cut the wire. The Dragonfly immediately flipped over to the right, splashing into the mud, and a startled 'Porky' suddenly found he was lying in shallow, muddy water still strapped in his seat, with his beloved camera immersed, alongside his nose. Clambering out of the wreck, soaking wet in his uniform, he furiously waded through the mud to await transport home, leaving his wrecked helicopter settling gently in the ooze. To say he was no longer his cheerful self is a massive understatement; his comments to the chastened Harness are not recorded but were unlikely to have been very polite.

Then, on the 15th, I was carrying out a routine flight off Port Stewart in Dragonfly 916 when we spotted one of our fisherman friends a mile or so offshore. As we flew close, the boat turned into wind and there was a man on the stern holding up a fish. Tempted by the bait, I descended towards the stern and Harness started to lower the basket with its customary gift of tins of aircrew emergency rations. At fifty feet I started to gently slip into the hover, to keep up with the boat. To my dismay the rotor revs fell away, and the hover became a continual descent into the sea. I just had time to make a Mayday distress call and we were in. As we ditched alongside the boat, I noticed the stunned man on the stern looking sideways at us, open mouthed, with his fish still held aloft. The boat was *The Girl Mary* and she reacted with commendable speed by circling round and coming up to our position. By now Harness and I were sharing my rubber dinghy in the swirl of bubbles left by the rapidly sinking 916. We were quickly pulled inboard, but there was some delay while the skipper went round again to rescue the dinghy; I think he had plans for it. I also thought that he would put in to Port Stewart, not very far away and, I discovered later, full of worthy citizens advising Eglinton of our plight, quite erroneously informing them that I had crashed into a fishing boat. The skipper then told me he was a 'Free State' boat and would not go in to an Ulster port. Instead he would land us back at his own harbour, Greencastle in Donegal. I was to find an hour or so later that he was a quick thinking man and well used to turning a disaster to some advantage. Greencastle was an hour or so away by fishing boat just inside the entrance to Lough Foyle. Soaking wet, we had to accept his decision and were, in due course, landed at Greencastle in Eire. Meanwhile, Eglinton had been in a flurry of activity arranging to obtain diplomatic clearance for an ambulance to come and pick us up.

As soon as we were ashore, still very damp, we were rushed from the jetty to the local bar and the skipper of *The Girl Mary* proudly, and loudly, declared us to be 'shipwrecked mariners'. This apparently entitled all involved to free drinks for resuscitation purposes and the excuse for a party to be held in the bar for the whole village; it hadn't escaped my notice that a surprising number of people were on the jetty to greet us as it became very apparent as to why the skipper came home to land us. By the time the ambulance arrived, we were ready for it. If it had taken any longer we would have needed it; sober but smelling strongly of rum, carrying a generous quantity of fresh haddock wrapped in newspaper, and to a chorus of fond farewells, we parted from our new friends. A few months later, Harness and I returned to Greencastle with a token of our appreciation. My father-in-law was a talented artist and he produced a large pastel drawing of *The Girl Mary* moored in her home port. I was pleased to present it to the delighted skipper in the bar, where the village enjoyed yet another excuse for a party.

The accident was attributed to a mechanical failure of the clutch drive between the engine and the main rotor, an unusual but known problem in the Dragonfly according to the engineers. With two SAR Dragonfly helicopters lost in November and later two Whirlwind Mk 7 helicopters lost later in December, sadly with one fatality, the aircraft accident statistics at Eglinton did not look too good that December.

As 1958 ended there was an air of uncertainty over station flight's future. 737 Squadron occupied the buildings next door to our offices for the purpose of training anti-submarine pilots destined for front line operations. They had, to date, been equipped with Gannet aircraft; but they were now replacing the Gannet with the new Whirlwind Mk. 7 anti-submarine helicopter coming into front line service. As 737 had now produced a crop of helicopter pilots, observers and their assistants also joined the squadron to become the nucleus of the next operational unit, 815 Squadron. Initially, the two squadrons were to share the squadron buildings with 737 as the Mk. 7 Whirlwinds arrived in numbers. They began to work up early in the year as a front line squadron and prepare for an eventual commission in a carrier

In our quiet little backwater we looked on with interest, but I was a trifle disturbed when the decision was made to absorb ship's flight into the new squadron. It indicated that moves were afoot to disrupt our cosy little unit. Jeremy left for pastures new and we obtained a Sub Lieutenant Tony Wilson in January 1959, to replace Jeremy. He was a newly appointed member of 815 but had also qualified on the Dragonfly and joined us for a month or so. I was instructed to convert to the Mk. 7 so that, with the exception of 'Porky,' who was now on the verge of retiring, we were capable of flying both types on SAR duties. I could understand that the greater lifting capability of the Whirlwind was essential. However, the new Mk. 7 helicopter was already gaining an unsavoury reputation; there had been several 'ditchings' and other emergencies. Also, as I had spent half of 1956 and most of 1957 on overseas commissions, I was reluctant to become involved with a front line squadron with all the implications of having to embark and leave my family once more. By March 1959, I had been finally induced to familiarize on the Mk. 7 and my logbook shows that on my second trip the engine seized up, luckily not while airborne. I cannot remember the details, so it could not have been a noteworthy event in the unhappy service life of the Mk. 7 helicopter. I flew the Whirlwind Mk 7 only three times.

RNAS Eglinton was now in the throes of closing down. 815 were due to leave for the new naval heliport, HMS *Osprey*, being constructed at Portland in Dorset as soon as it was completed. 'Porky' Meadowcroft had now retired, leaving me behind with Tony Wilson for company. Shortly after, in March, Tony flew one of our remaining Dragonflys to the holding unit at Fleetlands and then returned to Eglinton to join 815 to commence his anti-submarine helicopter training. With one helicopter, I was all that remained of the old station flight

Typical of the powers that be, the runway lighting and approach lighting had been in a state of decay since the war but now, with closure only months away, contractors had replaced all the lighting with the most up to date illumination possible. As there were no longer any fixed-wing aircraft left to do the calibration my last task at the air station was to fly the Dragonfly, carrying out fixed-wing circuit patterns, in order to calibrate the new approach lights. On 19 March 1959 I departed HMS *Gannet* for the last time to fly the longest helicopter flight of my career. With Harness and one other, we flew down to Fleetlands, a holding unit near Fareham in Hampshire, where aircraft of all sorts were refurbished or scrapped. It was a six hour flight via West Freugh, Silloth, Woodvale, Shawbury, Pershore and on to Fleetlands. I returned to Eglinton to collect my family and once again we moved back to the small apartment we maintained at Selsdon. I was however, not finished with the

Dragonfly or search and rescue duties. A few days later I joined the newly developing heliport at HMS *Osprey*, Portland, Dorset, as the SAR pilot. At this stage of construction there were no aircraft at the base, just Commander (Air), Commander Henley and myself, so there was nothing to fly for a week or so. I happily settled into Portland and helped with the administration and development as the base built up in order to operate anti-submarine squadrons later in mid-April, when 815 Squadron was to come down from Eglinton and take up residence at the heliport.

As a temporary detachment I joined the ship's flight of HMS *Victorious* from the end of April until the end of May to make up the numbers in the ship's Search and Rescue flight whilst she worked up in the Channel. On completion of this little interlude, I returned to Portland, to be instructed to collect a Dragonfly from Fleetlands, and set up the Portland SAR flight. In the meantime, in mid-April, 815 Squadron and its Whirlwinds had also moved from Eglinton to its new home at Portland and had commenced training anti-submarine helicopter crews in cooperation with the A/S frigates and submarines based at the Portland Naval base. This continued until July when they moved to RNAS Culdrose and 737 Squadron once more took over anti-submarine training at Portland. I was again under threat of being absorbed into the world of the Mk. 7. Happily I was left to my Dragonfly, as the SAR pilot until October

On the domestic front I managed to find a charming little cottage in Abbotsbury, a delightful old village by Chesil Beach and home to the famous Swannery and moved the family down to join me. Once again we were on a long list of applicants for a married quarter. It was a wonderful few months; a glorious summer and my duties were interestingly varied.

I flew all over the place on communication flights, taking various senior officers to meetings and I regularly flew beach patrols up and down the crowded beaches of Dorset. Without the squadrons to worry about I was frequently asked to assist the coastguard with searches as necessary. Two of note, were the rescue and transfer of a young lad on holiday at Lulworth with his parents. They reported that he had gone out for a walk the previous evening and not returned. The coastguard had searched the cliffs without success and, at daylight, requested a search by a helicopter. I searched the cliffs from the sea and soon discovered him. He had been stuck on a cliff all night, clear of the sea but under an overhang that prevented discovery from the cliff path above. I could not lift him because of the overhang but conned the coast guard for a cliff rescue and then landed in the car park at Lulworth to take the grateful but chilled lad to hospital for a check-up. The other incident involved a reckless threesome who, against advice, had gone outside the harbour at Poole in a small sailing dinghy in worsening conditions and were now unaccounted for. Again the coastguard requested our assistance to search the area together with the lifeboat. Amongst the 'white horses' I spotted something red. I found them adrift a mile or so off St Albans Head. As the wind had freshened, they were unable to hoist a sail and were distinctly uncomfortable, surrounded by an increasingly choppy sea. The two lads, with a distinct lack of chivalry, had used their female companion's red top to attract attention and she sat, in bra and shorts, shivering in the bow. Again, I was unable to help at all because of the wildly flailing mast. However I was in touch with the lifeboat, who was not too far away and by hovering near the now happier survivors, especially the girl, I guided the lifeboat to the dinghy's position.

On another occasion I was flying low down the beach from Lulworth to Portland when I noticed the paddle steamer *Daffodil* crowded with holiday makers on the regular excursion from Weymouth to Lulworth and return. She was on a course to pass close to me and before the skipper realized it, all the passengers, with their cameras clicking away, had rushed to the port side to get a photo of the Dragonfly. Whilst this was very flattering, it caused an alarming list in the *Daffodil*. The starboard paddle came out of the water and the poor skipper found himself 'underway but not under command', going in circles, with one wheel deep in the water, and the other one thrashing about in the air. I quickly flew off before I became involved in multiple rescues of *Titanic* proportions. I expect my side number was on many a happy holiday snap but luckily I heard no more. Again, I don't suppose that would be the outcome today.

Alas in late September my idyllic existence ended. At Culdrose 815 had reformed as the first operational helicopter anti-submarine squadron. Meanwhile 737 Squadron had been commissioned at Portland to take over the duty of training helicopter crews in the anti-submarine role and once again I was absorbed into the helicopter training with 737, destined eventually for front line service. A quick dual check with Lieutenant Pete Lines and my Dragonfly days were finally over and the SAR duties at Portland were taken over by 737 Squadron. I was now committed to the Whirlwind Mk. 7, for both anti-submarine and search and rescue duties. This helicopter was built by Westlands, with an Alvis Leonides Major engine specifically for the new role and was capable of hunting submarines by means of sonar. The helicopters, in groups, scanned a large area around the fleet by winching down the sonar gear operated by the observer and his rating assistant in the rear cabin. The submerged sonar sent out sonic pulses or 'pings' to reflect back off any submarine thereby giving its position. Listening skills had to be developed by the operators, as there are a host of underwater objects from wrecks to whales that can be mistaken for a submarine. It was my job to fly them to wherever they wanted to set up their pattern, and hold a hover over the spot until such time as they decided to move to listen in another area.

Within a very short time of its introduction, it had been found that the Mk. 7 had an intermittent but alarming problem in the engine. Because of the occasional nature, it was extremely difficult to trace the problem or eradicate it; the fault seemed to occur nearly always when hovering over the sea, although it is possible that it was not significant enough to be noticed in any less critical form of flight. Often whilst in the hover, the engine seemed to miss a beat and lose power. It was momentary but, being so close to the sea, frequently terminal to the flight. The aircraft sank into the water before the engine recovered. It was potentially lethal for the crews, especially those in the back; often there was no warning except the pilot's curse, and then they were struggling to get out as seawater surged in through their only exit. When ditching, the helicopter tends to roll over violently, especially when a rotor hits the water. Alarming for the pilot but not particularly threatening as he had excellent all round vision and easy escape facilities, but being disorientated suddenly made it much more difficult for anyone in the cabin to get clear of the sinking aircraft. I am amazed that fatalities were rare. I believe that as many as 60 per cent of all Mk. 7s produced, ditched, mainly due to this engine fault. Because there were so few aircraft recovered, it was very difficult to resolve the problem and many theories were put forward, but no cure. Much later, the most favoured theory was that the installation of the engine, and the rotation of the crankshaft in the Mk. 7 could cause a temporary oil starvation to the engine. I cannot say this was an aircraft that I warmed to; it was perfectly acceptable for most of the time but one always had to be aware when flying the beast, especially when hovering over the sea.

Once again, as the crews gathered at Culdrose to re-commission the new 815 Squadron, to my relief, I was left at Portland to continue search and rescue duties on behalf of 737 Squadron. This suited me very well, but I should have known my idyllic existence could not last. My name was known and I was now a fully trained anti-submarine pilot qualified on Whirlwind Mk. 7 helicopters.

Away from my naval duties, my wife and I were very happy living in our cottage at Abbotsbury, but there is never a guarantee with rented accommodation so I had entered my name on the list for a married quarter ever since joining Portland in April. I had never removed my name from the list. Busy on the anti-submarine course, the months slipped by without note. In mid-January, I was notified that an MQ had been allocated, so we moved into it at North Wyke, just across the Chesil Beach road from Portland, on the outskirts of Weymouth. Once again we were on the move and we left that charming village of Abbotsbury to start the whole business of settling into yet another new home. Such is the way for all servicemen and their families.

Chapter 13

Off Again – 815 Squadron

We had been in our new married quarter for less than three weeks and my house-proud wife had cleaned it from top to bottom. Hardly had we settled in when I had what was called a 'pier head jump'; an unexpected new appointment at very short notice. This was an emergency posting to make up the pilot numbers on a front line squadron. I had to pack and prepare to join HMS *Albion* in Malta on her way to the Far East; the squadron – my nemesis – 815. One of the 815 Squadron pilots had a wife who refused to accept that sea time was part and parcel of a Fleet Air Arm career. It would seem that she apparently pestered the Admiralty, even threatening suicide if he was not returned forthwith to her loving arms, and they conceded. Luckily, I did not see the man as I flew out to Malta to join on 4 March 1960. He had left the ship at Gibraltar, and I presume the Navy soon after. I later heard that on every previous embarkation, he had never passed Gibraltar. I must confess, I had been ashore since 1958, so I was probably on the books for a sea posting, but the reason for it annoyed me; I had never heard of such a trivial recall before. Their Lordships were not known for their compassion and most wives, having married into the Royal Navy, accepted that their menfolk would, at times, have to serve away from home.

I hurriedly packed and made my way to Stansted where I boarded a Dan-Air trooper plane to Hal Far, Malta. I was the only officer amongst a cargo of wives and children joining their menfolk in Malta. After a good flight, I descended into bright sunlight at Hal Far, the naval air station on the island. Other details are hazy with time but after catching some transport I was deposited at the dock to join HMS *Albion* for a second Far East cruise. My only consolation was that at least the deck landings should be a lot easier, and there would be no catapult launches to worry about in a helicopter. A quick re-familiarization flight and by 7 March, I was at sea and airborne with a new observer, Midshipman Rick Curtis. I had been allocated a cabin just under the flight deck, with Rick. We shared it with my old friend from Eglinton and the Dragonfly days, Tony Wilson, and his observer Brian Wakeman, also a midshipman. There was a good reason for crews to share a cabin as helicopters were often required at short notice for various tasks, and crew sharing meant that other members of the squadron were not too disturbed by a call-out. I was gradually getting used to being at sea again. HMS *Albion* had departed Malta within a day or two of my arrival for exercises in the Mediterranean en route to the Suez Canal. I felt an air of déjà vu as we departed Valletta for the East, just as I had done with 825 Squadron in 1956. Naturally I had immediately reported on my arrival to the commanding officer of 815 Squadron, Lieutenant Commander 'Knob' Cornabe. He had been appointed to command the squadron while it was at Culdrose so we had not met before. At the interview I found him to be unwelcoming and aloof. He pointed out how privileged I was to serve in his squadron and I felt that had he had a choice in the matter of appointment, I would not have been on the list. I did not ever discover his Christian name, and it certainly never occurred to me that it would be necessary to ask; after our introduction, I was sure that 'Sir' would suffice for any future conversation. After meeting his senior pilot, joint second-in-command of the squadron together with the senior observer, I knew that this commission was not going to be anything like my previous ones. There was a distinct social division, tacitly encouraged by the CO and senior pilot, between the few permanent commission general service officers and the short service officers, serving twelve years or less. It did not make for a happy squadron. Nevertheless, we were professional aviators and operationally we all rubbed along fairly well. In addition to our anti-submarine role, one crew was detailed each day for plane guard duties. They provided a safety helicopter at every launch or recovery of fixed-wing aircraft. Of course at any time we were available for a host of other tasks that could be carried out by the versatile rotary-wing.

Within a few days, while we were still within flying distance of Malta, there was a night flying programme for the fixed-wing aircraft. We were very aware of its progress as we lay in our bunks under the arrester wires on the deck above. Suddenly one of the bangs and crashes as a Sea Venom caught the wires was far louder than usual. Soon we were informed that a Venom had made a heavy landing, and then had carried on to slide over the side of the ship. There were apparently no survivors in the pitch dark sea, but we were instructed to prepare for a search of the area in the Whirlwinds at first light for the two missing aircrew. As dawn was breaking we launched all the available helicopters to carry out a low-level search of the area. After an extensive search, it was called off when a helicopter returned with some small pieces of plywood and fibreglass that were identified as being from a Sea Venom. It was all that remained of two young men and their aircraft. As is usual in these sad circumstances, the ship carried on with flying operations day and night, and the sombre business of packing the belongings of the men, was carried out by their comrades as, since before Nelson, the sad letters 'DD' – 'Discharged Dead' were entered against their records.

While off the North African coast, we were involved in an exercise with the Territorial Army. There was to be an operation involving dropping paratroopers in the Tobruk area. Lord Louis Mountbatten expressed his intention to observe the exercise, flying in helicopters from HMS *Albion* to the Army headquarters ashore. He was transferred to *Albion* and two helicopters ferried him and his staff to the tented headquarters of the troops destined to make the mock airborne assault. I was lucky enough to be one of the helicopter pilots chosen to fly some of his aides.

We landed at the HQ, situated in a very arid part of the desert, and shut down the helicopters. They now sat a little distance away shimmering in the sweltering sun, as we stood around to await the drop. Once on the ground, Lord Mountbatten was soon deep in discussion with senior Army officers; we chopper crews were only decoration, and we stood idly around, with a horde of junior Army officers, listening to the tactics and strategies being discussed by our seniors. Nothing seemed to be happening as the midday sun beat down. Then the word filtered down to us. The aircraft carrying the paratroops had missed the drop markers and dropped the unfortunate warriors some miles off target area. Their padre, luckily, was the only casualty; he had broken his ankle on landing. I wondered why the poor man had been so forsaken by his 'boss'. The unfortunate paratroopers were now faced with a long march back to where Lord Louis was to take the salute. I must confess I was glad it was them and not me.

As the staff talked to Army staff about what was to happen next, I became aware of a brass doorknob lying in the dust at Lord Mountbatten's feet. How odd, I thought; what is a tarnished old doorknob doing out here in the desert? It was obviously old, and this area had been an old battlefield so I brought it to the attention of my nearest Army colleague. After a quick look, he quickly bustled off and there was a slight flurry of activity in the tents. Lord Mountbatten was quietly shepherded away from the area. I don't think he even noticed the activity. Some NCOs quietly and very carefully removed the doorknob, and disposed off it in the small hills behind the camp. I heard a small thump, and I asked my new Army chum what the odd doorknob thing was. He replied that it was an Italian hand grenade left over from the war, and potentially 'live'. There were about thirty people gathered around Lord Louis, including me. I've sometimes pondered as to what effect it would have made to history if that thing had exploded.

Operation Starlight having been completed, with the Territorials presumably still marching back from their drop, without their injured padre, of course, we flew Lord Mountbatten back to *Albion* for transfer to his frigate and proceeded on our way to

Piraeus, Greece. There were just a few days to view the Parthenon and Acropolis and to be awed by the culture, comparing the timeless beauty to the perpetual dusty haze of modern Athens on the plain below. We were then off again on our way to transit the Suez Canal.

At one point, due to a misunderstanding between the captain and the Egyptian canal pilot, *Albion* struck the canal bank, causing some damage but not enough to prevent a swift passage to Aden. We only stayed a day or two to re-bunker the ship and show the flag. The helicopters were busy going to and fro, making excellent taxis. There was no leave at Aden as there were continuing terrorist problems, both in the city and the surrounding countryside. Not that there was much to attract the visitor. As we flew in and out, I thought that Aden was a grim, dusty place, with little to recommend it; it had a brooding air of malice.

We soon sailed for Singapore with 815 blissfully unaware of what lay ahead in the next few days. Flying took place nearly every day with the helicopters providing anti-submarine screens around the fleet. On 11 April I was on the first morning launch with four other helicopters to screen ahead of the carrier. There was hardly any wind and the sea was an oily calm, the most difficult conditions in which to hover at twenty feet above its surface. It is extremely difficult to gauge one's height over still, clear water, especially with only a slight breeze. As we entered the first hover my observer, Rick Curtis, lowered the sonar ball into the water. A minute or so later the Whirlwind gave the tiny shudder that some said indicated the engine was taking a brief rest. I applied full throttle but the rotor needle started to wind down as the twitching engine needle began to slowly regain its normal position. This happened faster than it takes to write, and my efforts to recover were of no avail. The Whirlwind slowly sank down into the water. Just before we entered, I managed to call a Mayday to the ship, who could, in fact, see our difficulties as we were only a mile or so ahead of her. It was a copybook ditching, if ever there can be such a thing. As soon as the rotor hit the water, there was a vicious rollover to the left leaving the aircraft practically inverted and barely afloat. All I had to do was undo my harness and exit sideways through the open door to my right. My main concern was for my crew in the rear cabin. On surfacing I saw Duffy, the telegraphist, floating in the water with a bent rotor blade tucked under his arm. Despite all safety briefings on surviving a ditching, in his eagerness to get clear of the sinking aircraft he had leapt out of the cabin prematurely, as the helicopter was entering the water, and rotors had stopped rotating. A rotating blade had carved up from underneath the fuselage and stopped just under Duffy's arm. A very lucky escape for Duffy, it emphasized the need to stay with the aircraft until everything stopped moving. Rick soon popped up and we all floated around for a while as the ship drew closer and the plane guard Whirlwind came to our rescue. I viewed its approach with a certain amount of suspicion. To be rescued from the water by the same aircraft type that had so recently dumped me unceremoniously into the Indian Ocean seemed to be rather tempting fate.

Freshly scrubbed and in a change of uniform, I contemplated my third A25 accident report, but worse for the whole squadron was to come. A signal came through grounding all Mk. 7s from further operations until 815 had carried out extensive hovering checks. For the next week or so the flight deck was covered in hovering Whirlwinds. We were instructed to throw them about, and agitate the fuel in the hope that one would fall back on deck and reveal the fault. It all looked like some bizarre, drunken aerial ballet, but without any positive results. With the problem unresolved, the squadron disembarked to Sembawang in Singapore and we continued our mad antics there, but still with nothing to work on. Given an all clear to resume normal operations, our helicopters were launched to take part in an anti-submarine exercise. The very first one to start a hover had the engine miss a beat. Luckily the sonar gear was not lowered and he still had forward speed. Apparently his wheels dragged through the water, but he made it safely back to Sembawang. Another Whirlwind, piloted by my old friend Tony Wilson, on the same sortie, lost power, also dragging his front wheels through the water, he too managed to get back to base on reduced power. His confidence battered, he made a running landing with what power he had and taxied back to the dispersal. With the problem still unresolved, the hovering tests were suspended, much to everyone's relief. It had been tedious, hovering all day, day after day, and we had proved nothing. However, the annoying fault seemed to subside for 815 Squadron from that date and we had no further problems on the commission from unexplained ditchings. Other squadrons though, continued to lose aircraft but the successor to the Mk. 7, the Westland Wessex, with a jet engine, was now beginning to come into operational service, and its successor, the Sea King, was already coming into service in the USA.

The end of April found 815 still disembarked at Sembawang while *Albion* carried out exercises at sea. She returned to Singapore in early May where she stayed until the 17th before sailing for Hong Kong, embarking 815 as she sailed north. A short stay at Hong Kong and we were off for Inchon in South Korea, exercising with an American taskforce, permanently based in the area to keep a watch on the fragile peace negotiated between North Korea and South Korea and their allies. We anchored off the port of Inchon and there was a flurry of helicopter activity serving the political demands of the visit. While we were there, all off duty officers were invited to a large cocktail party in Seoul. As we were part of a small fleet, this meant boats had to transport the partygoers to the harbour and they then travelled in coaches, supplied by the Americans, to the capital some distance away. It was interesting to see that the ravages of the Korean War were still very evident in 1960. The roads were pockmarked with bomb craters and all the many bridges were down, replaced by army Bailey bridges alongside them. Many buildings were the worse for wear but there was an extensive rebuilding programme in evidence.

The coach eventually arrived at a magnificent pavilion, resplendent with carved wooden dragons, and red and gold paint. No doubt due to the rich decoration, it reminded me of a huge fairground bumper car arena. It had originally been part of a large temple and, in accordance with tradition, anyone entering was required to remove their footwear. Already there was a large collection of assorted pairs of shoes neatly lined up on the many sets of steps leading up and into the pavilion. Some sixth sense warned me that there was scope for mischief in the unattended shoes and I persuaded my companions to conceal theirs under the steps, so that they were not so obvious.

Inside the party was in full swing and the drinks were both plentiful and generous in their measure; mostly spirits and of the best quality. It soon turned out to be a very jolly evening. As the party ended, we returned to our buses somewhat befuddled to begin the long, bumpy journey back to the ships. I was vaguely aware that there was some confusion among the guests, but our group found their shoes under the steps and departed on the ride back to the harbour. It was very late and most people, including myself, slipped into a dozy stupor only vaguely aware of the jolting ride in the coach. The next morning, rather thick headed and feeling unwell, I complained bitterly to my colleagues of the lack of consideration in not stopping at least once for a 'comfort break'. I was informed by unsympathetic friends who seemed to find it hilarious, that the bus had stopped several times for that very reason, but went on to thank me for protecting their footwear. Apparently two midshipmen observers on the Sea Venom squadron had mixed up all the visible shoes and many had to return shoeless to their ships, including some very un-amused but very senior officers. The two 'mids' were even now, at the command of the Admiral, rowing around the fleet in a small boat loaded with sacks, full of shoes, in an attempt to reunite them with their irate owners, together with their apologies. The weather was cold and damp and two abject midshipmen rowed back to *Albion* with several unclaimed pairs. They had learned that there are few better ways of getting very senior officers to remember your name. Needless to say, we were immensely amused by the incident, especially having escaped unscathed.

Our stay at Inchon was not a long one and, at the end of May 1960, we were exercising at sea en route to Japan. We arrived at

Yokohama around 9 June and came alongside the American Naval dockyard in Yokosuka for a period of self-maintenance on the carrier.

The post war presence of American forces in Japan was still very much in evidence and, as usual, they welcomed us with their customary hospitality. Mike Rayment, an observer on the squadron, and I, took up the offer made by the US Recreational Services, to spend a traditional weekend at a typical Japanese inn on the slopes of Mount Fujiama.

The established tradition of the old Japanese inn followed the premise that a bone weary traveller would arrive at the inn and fall exhausted from his pony, seeking shelter. Japanese hospitality demanded that he be stripped of his clothes by fair maidens and bathed in a relaxing, but nearly boiling bath, with water up to his neck. Parboiled, and well scrubbed, the traveller would be vigorously massaged by the maidens and finally kitted out with a large kimono and wooden slippers to pass the night, while his own clothing was laundered for the onward journey. So it was with Mike and me. After a long winding trip from Yokosuka up the mountain, we arrived at the old wooden inn in the middle of nowhere. The entire journey had been through countryside similar to the wilder, uninhabited parts of the Scottish Highlands including the swirling mist and constant steady rain.

It very quickly dawned on us that our hosts were unable to speak any English whilst our Japanese was limited to 'suki yaki' and 'sayonara'. Our room was apparently constructed of paper and bamboo with a highly polished floor; two cushions and a low table were its only furnishings. Scrubbed red and pummelled, we were left glowing by our silent, bowing maids, to explore our simple room. Through the window, the rain poured in a tumbling, rocky torrent over which our room was precariously perched. There would be no moonlight flit from this place. There was nothing Mike or I could do but sit crossed legged on the pair of cushions and compare our plight to that of a Trappist monk. We found that the deep square bath, mysteriously continuously filled with very hot water, so that it was always available for bathing tired limbs. The afternoon passed extremely slowly. With a timid knock, our two maids appeared with dinner. On two individual trays, it was set on the low table. The first course set the tone. It was a small trout like fish, anguished eyes bulging and twisted in rigor mortis; it looked as if it had been thrown alive into whatever cooked it. Appetite diminished by guilt, we picked at it, and patiently waited for the silent service to bring the second course. It was a very tasty suki yaki, to be followed by a delicious looking dessert of what looked like pink cubes of Turkish delight and marshmallow in a creamy sauce. Unfortunately it turned out to be cubes of raw fish in a sour curd. After little discussion, we made arrangements to leave the next day after breakfast.

Dinner over, we decided we must explore whatever delights were available in the public rooms. We soon found that we were the only guests and the staff had vanished; we were apparently alone in the inn. The choice of entertainment lay between table tennis, a game that proved absolutely impossible in a kimono and wooden sandals, or pool, of which we knew nothing, and were unlikely to find any instruction we could understand. We settled for TV, and spent a hilarious hour watching a Japanese-speaking Marshal Matt Dillon aided by a shrill voiced Japanese Dillon, taming a wild west town full of Japanese desperados.

Our hosts, obviously upset at our poor appetites, provided a full American breakfast for us the next morning. Disastrously, it had been prepared the previous evening and stored carefully in the refrigerator overnight. I can assure any reader that icy, cold fried egg on chilly bacon with cool soggy toast, is every bit as awful as cubes of raw fish in sour curd. We gratefully boarded our bus and returned to the carrier, and the comforts of home.

Another strange experience was my unexpected selection as officer in charge of the shore patrol. With the harbour bars awash, filled with hard drinking sailors from all the ships of the combined fleet, it was felt that we should support the US Naval police patrols policing this potential trouble spot. Apart from me in full white dress uniform and rather oddly, armed only with a whistle, I led a petty officer and six ratings, equally oddly armed with brand new pickaxe handles. They were also dressed in best whites and shiny black gaiters. I could not help feeling we were a bit under-equipped. A trifle self conscious, we left the ship for the American police headquarters.

We found the Americans in khakis and white helmets and carrying a variety of automatic pistols, sub-machine guns and long batons. They were vastly amused by my patrol, dressed in virginal whites and so lightly armed. They thought we were rather cute, especially in our shiny black gaiters. They seemed to think that our effect on any rioting, drunken sailors would leave them powerless to resist arrest as they rolled hysterical with laughter on the ground.

Soon after we arrived at the Police HQ, we found we were to join them on a raid on a source of pornographic material. An inebriated American rating had been arrested and strip-searched before we arrived. The searchers discovered that the rating, a native American improbably called Hoot Owl, had a strip of pornographic film hidden in his sock. The American lieutenant, expressing disgust, held the strip of film up to the light to show me the scenic evidence. Perhaps my life had been too sheltered but I could not make out what was in the frames of the small strip of film, and neither could my much more experienced, lascivious stokers, jostling their officer for a better view. Led by our American hosts we piled into the black and white patrol cars and hurtled off, blue lights flashing, to the address given by the incoherent Hoot Owl, now sleeping it off in a cell.

In a quiet suburb on the side of a steep hill, we puffed and wheezed up about 300 steps, lamely following the American patrol as they raided the pornographic dealer's house with impressive fitness, efficiency and a startling ferocity. It was 1 a.m. and suspiciously quiet. My patrol was, by now, looking rather dishevelled and sticky, our 'whites' crumpled and stained by our steamy exertions. Still keen, the Americans stormed the house, bursting down doors to gain entry to this den of iniquity.

An elderly, scared Japanese couple cowered inside and, by the time the Royal Navy arrived to add to the confusion, it had been found to be the wrong address. Terrified by the Americans, our pathetic arrival pacified them somewhat; as we collapsed, sagging wearily onto our pickaxe handles, they were anxiously gazing at us with timid smiles, and trying to revive us by offering small cups of tea. They recognized a comedy show when they saw one.

I don't know what happened to the hapless Hoot Owl when he sobered up, but I would guess it was some time before he saw the 'happy hunting grounds' again. We returned to *Albion* only too pleased to get rid of the whistle, pickaxe handles and shiny black gaiters, thankful that there were no members of our ship's crew sharing Hoot Owl's accommodation.

At the end of June HMS *Albion* left Japan for Hong Kong and Singapore. There was a certain elation throughout the ship as we were now at the start of the long voyage home. Every nook and cranny was stuffed with the presents and curios that we had purchased in the mysterious East. Even as we gently rolled south in the China Sea and onwards, we exercised continuously with the accompanying fleet, carrying out the varied tasks allotted to helicopters and their crews, from anti-submarine screens to taking mail and fresh bread to the smaller frigates and submarines. Surprisingly enough the Mk. 7 gave no further trouble, although we were still no wiser about the engine fault that caused the ditchings earlier in the year. However, we were still hearing of other squadrons who were plagued with the problem and the poor Whirlwind's reputation had not improved.

By early June we were alongside in Singapore where we were to stay until the end of July for dockyard maintenance. During the stay, two of our pilots, Tony Wilson and Bill Flynn, were transferred at short notice to 848 Squadron in the Royal Marine Commando Support Carrier HMS *Bulwark*. She must have been short of pilots and was urgently required for operations in Kenya. They were not to rejoin us until mid-September, having had some very different adventures with the Royal Marine Commandos in the African bush.

In the meantime, after a further visit to Subic Bay in the Philippines, the ship was busy exercising in the China Sea when, sadly, yet another of the Sea Venoms was lost during night-flying exercises when it crashed into the sea on take-off.

Following this we enjoyed a brief visit to Hong Kong before returning to Singapore, arriving to disembark the helicopters to operate from Sembawang until the homeward voyage recommenced in October.

A nine-day stay in Ceylon, visiting Colombo and Trincomalee, presaged a short visit to Karachi for briefings for the major maritime exercise, Exercise Midlink 3, which was to take place with the naval forces of the CENTO countries. This was a period of intense operations which came as close as possible to simulating a war situation without any actual shots being fired, and very hot and sweaty it was too.

After a brief return to Karachi to debrief the results of our exercise the ship sailed to Mombasa for a period of 'rest and relaxation' and the acquisition of yet more souvenirs. On 29 November we set off, homeward bound, having completed our commission to the Far East.

We were now definitely bound for the UK. In the best traditions of travel documentaries, the little red track plodded relentlessly through the Suez Canal and into the Mediterranean Sea where we pitched and rolled in the ferocious storms that welcomed us to more northern climes. For a while, we stood by HMS *Victorious*, a large fleet carrier that had a problem with jammed rudders and could only keep way on by going in circles. As she turned through the violent seas, there was always a potential for broaching and even capsizing. Luckily, after a few worrying hours the problems were resolved and we continued on our way. On 16 December 1960, 815 Squadron disembarked the aircraft to the holding and refurbishment unit at Fleetlands near Gosport. Our Far East commission was over and, after collecting our kit from the ship and saying farewell to our colleagues, we all proceeded on leave for the Christmas break. Joining instructions were already in my pocket for my next appointment. A very interesting posting to

RNAS Yeovilton awaited me, as a trials and development pilot with 700 Squadron in 1961.

I cannot say that the 815 Squadron that I joined in 1960 was ever a happy squadron. That, of course, may not be a recognized requirement of a military unit but it does help morale. Unfortunately the squadron officers were divided by an 'us and them' attitude, promoted by the commanding officer and his senior pilot. There was a distinct aloofness by the Dartmouth trained officers and very little mingling with the short service entry pilots and observers in a social way. Although this in no way affected the operational role of the squadron, I felt that the unit never melded properly and had none of the camaraderie of the other squadrons. I left HMS *Albion* without a backward glance, job done, having made only a few friends. Then, forty years later, I met up with an old colleague, Tony Wilson, with whom, together with our observers, I had shared a noisy, hot, cabin underneath the most popular arrester wire in the *Albion*. When aircraft recovery was in progress, they thumped down on our 'ceiling', or deckhead, to give it its correct naval name, with a horrendous crash and scraping sound as the wire caught the hook and then returned to the ready position, whilst showers of flaked paint fluttered down on us from above.

Tony had contacted the 'Lost and Found' column in a Saturday edition of the *Daily Mail* newspaper, seeking news of his ex-observer, Brian Wakeford. Seeing this entry, I discovered that he had retired to the South Hams, not too far from me and arranged a meeting that has firmly cemented, in old age, a friendship that originated in the late 1950s.

Chapter 14

Trials and Development – Whatever Next?

I entered the squadron offices in eager anticipation after the Christmas break of 1960. After I had made my number with Tony Shaw, the commanding officer, he introduced me to the other helicopter pilot on the squadron, Lieutenant Colin Moorcraft. Colin had been on the upperyardman section of the course ahead of me at Syerston so I already had a nodding acquaintance with him. After the formalities Colin took me over to the hangar to show me the aircraft that we would be using to evaluate new equipment, prior to any contract being placed with the manufacturer. In the helicopter section we were to fly a variety of Whirlwind marks. There were also three other small helicopters of a type I had never seen before. Colin explained that they were P531s, a prototype, and we would be carrying out extensive trials, together with testing equipment to suit the roles in which they were expected to perform. It was anticipated that they would operate from small ships to provide an extended range to the ships' attack systems, both anti-submarine and surface systems. They would also be invaluable in all the other functions of the fleet helicopter. They still carried the prototype numbers allocated by Saunders-Roe as they had developed them for their prospective users, the Royal Navy and the Army Air Corps. Subject to the Admiralty decision after evaluation by 700

Squadron, if they were eventually purchased by the Services, they were to be named the Wasp in the naval role and the Scout for the Army.

For the immediate future, I was to be involved in the current trials using an American Mk. 3 Whirlwind adapted to assess a minesweeping role for helicopters. Colin said that, together with another pilot, Mike Fournel, we would take the aircraft down to Portland on the morrow and introduce me to the 'gentle' art of minesweeping in the bay between Weymouth and Lulworth; familiar ground for me. Furthermore, Mike was soon to leave the squadron, to take up another appointment, and I would take over the trial from him. It all sounded fascinating. I sauntered over to the Whirlwind and saw with amazement that the cabin was virtually filled with a huge reel of black rubber cable that must have been four inches in diameter. It filled the cabin almost completely and must have weighed as much as the helicopter. The last time I had seen, or used this equipment, was on the ill-fated minesweeper *1044*. It was a monstrous piece of gear then, and age had not withered it. The principle of its use was exactly the same as on the minesweeper. In this case the cable, as thick as an arm, was streamed through a hole in the cabin floor. When fully extended in the sea and trailing slowly astern, all 100 yards of it, a substantial electric current was passed through it to magnetize it. This was supposed to simulate the magnetic field normal in any ship. The magnetic field would trigger the detonator of the mine. It immediately occurred to me, that if a mine were already waiting in situ under the chopper when the current was switched on, we would be the first flying machine to be sunk by an underwater explosion. I should mention that, at this stage we were assessing the practical possibility of towing the cable at all.

The next day I flew the Mk. 3 down to Portland to practise sweeping in Weymouth bay. Of course, there was nothing to sweep; but the technique to do so required some unusual flying that I reckoned was right on the edge of the Whirlwind's performance limit. The method developed by my colleagues was to fly slowly in a straight line streaming the cable. Once the cable was in the water, the helicopter was firmly attached to the sea and pulling the equivalent of a small ship. This heavy drag meant that in order to maintain straight and level flight, you had to fly with the rudder pedals, controlling the tail rotor, continuously held with one leg fully extended, and the other fully bent, with the knee almost resting on the instrument panel. This, in itself, was wearisome but the control column had to be firmly pushed over to one side and forward with maximum power kept on, to keep airborne. I think that possibly a yoga expert may have a word for the position the unfortunate pilot had to adopt while towing what seemed like a dead whale through the sea at about 10 knots. If it had ever been brought into service, aircrew would have had to be recruited from the trucking fraternity. After about thirty minutes, a second pilot was required to take over. I always thought from the outset that it was a precarious occupation and physically exhausting. I would not dispute that it was a good idea; and it was now my job to evaluate such ideas during my time on the squadron.

After a few days struggling slowly across the bay I thought that later more powerful helicopters might perform the task satisfactorily, with power assisted controls but as it existed in its present form I could not give the project my personal recommendation. Minesweeping was quietly shelved; I did not have to produce any trial reports on it but I am sure that my views would have been similar to those of my colleagues, and I think that by the time I appeared on the scene, a negative decision had already been made to shelve helicopter mine-sweeping.

My next task was to familiarize myself with the P531. Colin took me up for an introduction flight on 23 January 1961, followed by a solo flight forty minutes later. The P531 was a feisty little helicopter, mostly a Plexiglas cabin for two aircrew seated side-by-side. The small fuselage also housed a Blackburn turbo-jet engine. It would have reminded any pilot who had trained on the little Hiller helicopters of being in an advanced version of that sporty, exciting machine. Being destined for use on small frigates, its development schedule revolved around suitable equipment, mainly for hunting submarines and associated weaponry. Evolving an acceptable landing gear, suitable for the limited landing area available on the stern of a frigate, were the considerations at present. The particular problems to be solved initially related to landing the helicopter safely from every flight on the severely restricted confines of the stern area. Obviously any serious slippage could easily lead to the aircraft toppling over the side of the frigate and possibly causing injury to deck crew in the worst instance. It was therefore imperative that some sort of undercarriage, that would give a safe and positive adhesion on a slippery, possibly violently moving deck, was needed and we were the pilots to slip and slide until a suitable solution was accepted. The first selections brought forth were four non-slip pads, thought to be suitable. They were now being designed and were shortly to be available for practical testing. We had a date for a trial at sea with HMS *Undaunted*, a frigate with a converted stern, able to take a helicopter. They were to take place at the end of April into May, and we were to prepare earlier than that with two days' rehearsal at the Royal Aircraft Establishment, Bedford, making use their 'rolling deck'. If the dry runs were successful, we would cross the Irish Sea with one P531 to RAF Ballykelly. There we would refuel the aircraft before flying on to land on HMS *Undaunted*. Colin and I were to be the pilots. Until that date, there was plenty of evaluation on other projects to be carried out.

I should point out that, as trials and development pilots, we were only required to test equipment and its suitability for use by a future operational pilot. Observers evaluated any equipment pertaining to the observer role, but they always needed drivers.

I had to get to know the P531 well before the trials. In addition to this I had other tasks, mostly testing new equipment for use by observers, using our Whirlwinds and a lone Dragonfly that we had to play with. Fortunately, minesweeping was no longer on the schedule.

The P531 proved to be a feisty little helicopter. Powered by a turbo-jet engine, it was easier to start than piston engine models. Once in the air it was surprisingly quiet and smooth to fly, just a high-pitched scream coming from the power unit. Being small and with the cockpit having a bubble glass around it, it gave excellent all round vision and a feeling that you were suspended in the air. The aircraft was very nippy and as responses by the aircraft appeared to take place so quickly, the mind and reflexes were, not surprisingly, concentrated. It was more akin to a racing car than a military project. Of course at this stage, it was a pure rotary wing aircraft such as a disc jockey or A-list celebrity might purchase. The only modifications made to the P531 as a military aircraft were those that allowed us to quickly install or remove the various items of equipment that we were assessing for a particular task; once fitted out for the roles expected of it at sea, its increased weight would inevitably slow it down. I resolved to enjoy the sensation of unencumbered flight while I could. The racehorse could rapidly become a carthorse in the military aviation world; every aeronautical designer had something they wished to hang on any new aircraft.

One thing slightly worried me. I was told that Saunders-Roe, the manufacturers, had been reluctant to release the helicopter to the Navy for trials use, as the three helicopters had all nearly reached the end of their programmed flying life. They had been extensively flown by Saunders-Roe on demonstrations and at air shows. Somehow, a way around this hurdle had been found and now, possibly past their sell-by-date, here they were for us to play with. Naturally Saunders-Roe were interested in the various trials that we had scheduled for their prototype and provided us with all the help they could to maintain the P531.

After a week or so, my general flying practice and familiarization was complete and I was deemed qualified to undertake any trial that was considered necessary in the process of acceptance of a production model into fleet service. Meanwhile there were other calls on our time to complete trials on various devices that fitted into Whirlwinds. I was in my element flying different aircraft on such a variety of tasks. Records showed a fascinating history of the squadron from the beginning of the war. Every sort of aircraft, from captured enemy types to the ever improving models that came into fleet service, or were thought to offer potential, were flown and evaluated. Since well before the war, all the famous aircraft manufacturers had supplied machines to the squadron for assessment; the records made fascinating reading.

One of the many things now being evaluated was a new navigational system. I think it had been based on a navigation aid fitted in shipping, designed and produced by Decca, mainly for coastal or short range confirmation of the user's position. It consisted of master stations and slave stations situated ashore around the coast. They automatically transmitted ranges and bearings that could be received and plotted onto a chart. Where any number of bearings crossed, gave the position of the user. It had obviously been scaled down to make it a viable aid in an aircraft. It had an enviable reputation for accuracy, with instances of ships, in bad visibility, colliding because they were travelling in opposite directions using the same range ring to position themselves.

Fitted in a Whirlwind, I carried out several flights with an observer, Jim Bradley. With me flying the Whirlwind blind, with a cloudy plastic screen that blocked reference outside the helicopter, attached to my helmet, I flew for quite long periods around the Somerset countryside using only my instrument panel to navigate the aircraft and Jim's instructions on courses to steer and speeds to fly. I was always very impressed when we took off blind and over an hour later, landed within feet of our departure point. I did not ever hear of this equipment being used, probably because satellite navigation, just as accurate but more importantly, worldwide in its application, was already coming into use. That is one of the frustrations of trials work. By the time a piece of modern technology is evaluated, something better has been developed, and is often half the price.

At the end of April 1961 Colin and I took the P531 up to RAE Bedford for the initial 'rolling deck' trial. The Royal Aircraft Establishment had created a mock-up of an area the size of a frigate's deck and mounted the platform on a frame that looked like scaffolding. They had devised an ingenious motorized system that rolled the platform in a similar way to the stern of a frigate. Seen from the ground it looked alarming when gyrating around; the platform, our flight deck, being about thirty-five feet above the ground and rocking and rolling like some fairground ride. The P531 was fitted with what the boffins had dreamed up as the answer to the problem of stopping slippage after landing on a very restricted, probably wet, violently moving deck. On each skid there were two circular plates containing ridged rubber discs. All Colin and I had to do was to carry out thirty-six deck landings each, on the rolling deck, for the inventors to see if it was a viable answer before repeating the trial on board a real frigate, moving on a hopefully boisterous, real sea. The powers that be had already decided that HMS *Undaunted* would be the frigate, and the usually frisky Irish Sea off Londonderry the venue.

Landing on the Bedford deck was a novel experience. Once over the deck there was little visible reference available to the heaving platform below. A slow descent from the hover, until some part of the skid touched the deck and then a decisive landing worked well although both Colin and I noted that the P531 could 'waltz' about on its rubber pads at first contact. It was advisable to be ready for a quick lift off if the movement became too pronounced. However, our thirty-six landings satisfied the assembled inventors who, incidentally, stood well away from the heaving contraption to observe the experiment. The trip to HMS *Undaunted* was confirmed for early May. The really interesting part of the trial was yet to come.

In early May we joined HMS *Undaunted* with P351 and a ground crew and, on the 5th, started our deck landing trials. The weather was extremely disappointing. Unusual for the Irish Sea, it was flat calm, with a sluggish swell. Nevertheless, I managed a few deck landings with no trouble at all. It was rather inconclusive as the ship was so steady, I could have been landing ashore, having the ship's superstructure to refer to. It was certainly easier to land on than the 'deck' at Bedford. After conferring with the captain, it was decided that they would try to induce a more realistic movement by going at full speed and making the ship roll by continually reversing the helm. From the air, it looked as if the man at the wheel was drunk and it must have been uncomfortable for all on board. Colin and I made several approaches to the now rolling deck and landed on. The 'waltzing' of the aircraft across the deck noted at Bedford was far more evident but not dangerous. Over the next few days we continued the trial and discovered that the bouncing around was becoming much more evident and at times alarming. It was discovered that the movement, together with the slip resistant gritty paint on the flight deck, had badly eroded the rubber pads on the skids. With a wet deck, there was hardly any adhesion at all. Disappointed, we completed other trials relevant to future small ship operations before returning to Yeovilton to discuss alternative, more durable undercarriages for the helicopter. A tethering device was mooted that once attached, winched the aircraft down onto the deck and castor like wheels that could be locked at an angle and so prevent any wayward movement on landing. Of course these methods were not immediately available and although I was not to know it, my deck landing days with the P531 were soon to cease forever.

For the present however, we had other trials to occupy our time back at RNAS Yeovilton. Much later, in 2008, at the 815 Squadron gathering at Yeovilton, I met a pilot who had served in a frigate with an operational Wasp. He declared it to be '...the finest little helicopter he'd ever flown in'. I felt proud to have been involved in its development.

The next project for the P531 was the evaluation of some submarine detection equipment. Another Colin, Lieutenant McClure an observer, was to carry out the trial while I did the flying. The device entailed towing a small, light glider-like receiver at the end of a long cable streamed from the back of the aircraft. Colin faced backwards alongside me, operating the display. We had been told that this lightweight and compact apparatus had been developed by the American oil industry to discover oilfields from the air. The US Navy had realized its military potential and much to the oil firm's chagrin, and their own reluctance, allowed us to borrow one of the valuable kits to carry out our own tests in our lightweight helicopter. Its rarity and value had been stressed and its safe return emphasized by our American allies. If we could operate it successfully, it would make an ideal submarine detection package for the new Wasp. The preliminary trials proceeded satisfactorily and Colin McClure and I detached from Yeovilton to Portland in late June 1961, to carry out further trials to locate known wrecks lying in the seas off Chesil Beach. The seabed was liberally scattered with well-charted wrecks and our hopes were high. If we could not find them, the project would be considered a failure.

Chapter 15

A Tragic Conclusion

We had been flying for several days in June without getting the positive results we had hoped for. There had been enough to encourage further testing and Colin and I took off at midday to fly down Chesil Beach towards Charmouth. The area was strewn with known wrecks. It was perfect weather on 19 July 1961 and, as was fairly usual for helicopter crews, we flew, relaxed, in our uniforms instead of the regulation flying suit. Colin was sitting at his controls operating the equipment, facing backwards as we flew out to the tip of Portland Bill, maintaining 300 feet. Turning onto a westerly course, I streamed the receiver on its cable, behind the aircraft. I settled on the course given to me by Colin and, as is usual when working gear, we remained silent except for any flight alterations required by Colin. I casually noted a frigate close inshore by the beach passing down my starboard side. It was virtually stationary and I assumed it must be taking a break from its exercises to carry out the more important 'up spirits', when grog is issued.

There was a slight bang and my controls went slack, immediately the helicopter reared up and rolled over out of control. Realizing that we were in serious trouble, I quickly called a Mayday. By now we were descending fairly rapidly and whirling round and round, gyrating violently as we did so. I thought that the tail rotor must have failed in some way, as the fuselage was now trying to equate with the main rotor revolutions by spinning madly in the opposite direction. I ordered Colin to jettison his side door and, in case he was still in doubt, told him we were about to ditch. As we were pitching and rolling so much, the sea view only occasionally passed by the windscreen followed by blue sky and glimpses of land flashing by. I fought to try and regain some form of control, as I had read of a similar incident that had been resolved by keeping the helicopter in forward flight, the airflow keeping it relatively stable. It was painfully apparent that the P531 had never read this article.

Inevitably, we finally ditched into the sea with a teeth jarring crash and, I should think, a huge splash. Without the doors, we sank immediately, filling swiftly with water, but at least with the doors jettisoned, it was possible to unstrap and roll sideways out of the wrecked helicopter, now sinking rapidly, intent in joining the rusting hulks that we had been seeking only a minute or so ago. Totally immersed I rolled free of the helicopter, by now well down into the dark depths. Disorientated and not knowing the way to the surface, I inflated my life saving waistcoat and floated to the surface. Thanks to all the adrenalin, I was unaware of any injuries. Once at the surface, I looked around for Colin and was dismayed to see no sign of my friend. With only your head floating at the surface it is often difficult to see beyond the next wave and I desperately hoped I would see his head bobbing nearby. As I turned around seeking him, I saw a rescue boat approaching me from the frigate. They, of course, had been astounded witnesses to the whole event. They hauled me into the boat and onto a stretcher, with me anxiously telling them of the missing Colin and asking them to search. The sea was fairly calm but they could find nothing on the surface. By now the adrenalin had subsided and, as feeling returned, it was obvious to me that I had some slight injuries. On impact my mouth had been open, probably cursing; having slammed shut, it felt as if I had damaged some teeth; my right shoulder felt badly bruised and I had pain in my lower back that was now rapidly getting worse. When I complained of this in the boat they sensibly, but painfully, turned me onto my stomach and I was lifted onto the frigate in this most undignified position.

While the ship hastily returned around the Bill to Portland, the surgeon on board, armed with a pin, checked to find out whether I still had feelings in my legs. My affirmatives, through teeth now clenched with pain, reassured him, and me, that there was no paralysis. Little enough comfort as I thought of my lost observer, Colin, but by now the intense, steadily increasing pain in my back was taking most of my attention.

An ambulance met the frigate, HMS *Troubridge*, as she docked and I was carefully loaded aboard having thanked those who had been so conveniently able to give assistance. The loaded ambulance made its way slowly over the cobbles of the naval base, every slight jarring causing great spasms of agony in my lower back; even just thinking about it hurt. Arriving at the civilian Portland hospital, I was whisked up to the X–ray department where a stern faced nursing sister ordered me to lie face down on a table that was nearly chest high. I tried to tell her that with my back problems it was impossible to climb onto a high table but she would have none of it and, in agony, I somehow managed to clamber onto it, muttering darkly through gritted teeth.

The X-rays showed that I had bad compression fractures of two lower vertebrae. Luckily, I was now in the care of the Portland civilian hospital with one of the best specialists in spinal injuries in the south-west taking an interest. Mr Hywel-Davies later that day came into my side ward to talk over the results of the X-rays. Apparently the impact of the crash had crushed two lumbar vertebrae into wedge shapes, fortunately not causing any damage to the nerves in and around the area. He enquired about my sporting activities and when I mention my history as a hooker in various rugby teams, he advised me that luckily, I had very strong back muscles that would support me into the future, but the injuries were permanent and would result in a weakened back with a varying measure of back pain for the rest of my life. There was nothing that he could do for the present but advised that bed rest would ease the healing process. Then a group of naval officers came in and sat around the bed. I could not help thinking it must resemble the famous painting *The Death of Nelson*, but didn't say anything in case it caused laughter and I could not bear to even think of the pain that would induce. I dreaded sneezing or coughing as any movement at all created breathtaking spasms. The naval people wanted to confirm my earlier report on the ditching position, as it was imperative to recover the secret equipment and the equally important wreck of the P531 before other interested but unwelcome parties arrived on the scene; a salvage vessel had already left Portsmouth for the area. Meanwhile the search for Colin had not found any sign and it was thought that he was still with the aircraft. I was then left staring at the ward ceiling wondering what I could have done to change things.

My ever supportive wife rushed down from Yeovilton that evening to visit me, a stalwart life member of that band of ladies whose husbands are employed in perilous occupations.

The next day I was told that the wreck of the P531 had been located and salvaged. Colin was sadly still with the aircraft, it was thought that the equipment we were testing had broken loose from its temporary mountings on impact and stunned him; facing backwards, a foot had also been trapped in the helicopter's structure. It was a tragic ending for a pleasant, quiet officer who was looking forward to returning to civilian life in a few weeks' time. Later, the captain of HMS *Osprey*, the Portland base hosting us, took my wife down to the airbase to see the wreckage, now landed from the salvage ship. She was appalled at the sight of the helicopter. In twenty-four hours the sea had corroded the thin aluminium of the coachwork to a web of holes. The wreck was crumpled and difficult to recognize as a flying machine, the twisted pilot's seat had a torn, gaping hole where control junctions underneath had burst through like an artillery shell; the cause of my back injury was dramatically obvious. It has remained an awful memory for her to this day.

However, the whole aircraft, including the jettisoned doors, detached tail rotor and the gear we were towing, had been brilliantly and totally recovered in very difficult conditions. Unfortunately, the sea had consumed nearly every bit of the equipment and I was told that our unhappy American cousins had taken back only a handful of brass gearwheels. Later, when I saw the wreckage of the P531, I noted the cause of my injury; on impact with the sea, my seat had collapsed to the floor. Beneath the seat there was a large metal joint connecting several controls together. This irregular shaped joint about the size of a grapefruit had driven through my seat-pan like an armour piercing shell. The seat cushion and dinghy pack had prevented any actual wounding from the torn metal, but the impact had been transmitted up the spine causing the compaction.

A few days later a group of Saunders-Roe experts and naval advisors gathered around my bed to discuss, and listen to a bent pilot's views on a possible resolution to any future accident where a Wasp or Scout might 'ditch'. I listened in dawning horror as they proposed fitting flotation bags behind the cockpit and just under the main rotors. An immersion switch would automatically inflate them once in the water and keep what was left of the aircraft afloat, while the hapless crew evacuated the partially submerged 'goldfish bowl' of a cockpit. It occurred to me immediately that the position of the bags under the rotors would, in the first instance, according to Sod's Law, inflate and damage the main rotor while the aircraft was airborne and going peaceably about its business. Of course this was a mere pilot's view, and all but me insisted that this would never happen. They did say however, that they would consider my opinion and I am glad to say that production models had flotation bags attached to the undercarriage. Better to float upside down on the surface, rather than fall from several hundred feet without main rotors, remains my humble end user's view.

Mr Hywel-Davies visited nearly every day, insisting that I lay on my now familiar hard board but allowing me to do whatever my back pain would permit. I was not allowed the use of any supports, such as crutches or similar aids as he felt that they would become an essential and obscure the true recovery. Naturally, as I felt more able to move about, I disagreed with him but was in no position to argue. In fact, I now know he was absolutely right. Fourteen days later I walked out of the hospital to go back to Yeovilton. True, I shuffled with a strange, tensed, upright stance that involved a lot of sharp hisses and gasps but at least I was mobile again thanks to his care. I was then transferred to the care of the naval medical staff, on light duties until, as and when, I felt able to climb into a uniform again.

Oddly enough, although I was in the care of naval medical services at Yeovilton, I was required to make regular visits up to the naval hospital at Haslar, Gosport. This meant that several times I had to make the painful, inconvenient journey in my car to see the consultant. Nearly every time, it was just a ten-minute affair enquiring how I felt and then I was on the long journey home again. I was left to my own devices to wander about the station helping out where I could, doing ground tests on helicopters or various administration duties. One of my problems was that I could not stay in one position too long and had to stand up or sit down every few minutes, generally fidgeting about in order to avoid backache. After about six months my visit to Haslar ended with a discussion as to what I should do in the future. I was medically advised that the choice was mine but that I must bear in mind that the permanently damaged vertebrae meant that any flying that might lead to a heavy landing or a similar down force could easily lead to sideways movement of the wedge-shaped bones, taking the spinal cord with them and causing paralysis. After consideration of all aspects, especially the prospect of being crippled, with a young family, this bleak option meant the end of my flying career in the Services. Because of the permanence of the injury, obtaining insurance to fly professionally would be difficult and the cost prohibitive, also future employment in civilian flying would be very unlikely. After a little thought, I elected to transfer to air traffic control duties until the end of my twelve-year commission. At least I would still be in the world of aviation. In a very introspective mood, I returned to Yeovilton to wait for the 'wheels' of the naval appointees to grind out a new appointment to attend the air traffic control course.

Chapter 16

Someone Has to Do It

Early in 1962, I was appointed to RAF Shawbury to join the combined services air traffic control course, pending a transfer to the ATC branch of the Navy. Having spent the last few weeks getting a feel for it in the tower and radar rooms at Yeovilton, I was not exactly overjoyed at the prospect. From what I had seen, air traffic control seemed to be a quiet, even boring occupation, with long periods when there was little or nothing to do. I very soon discovered that every hour or so, the whole tower had thirty minutes of frenetic activity when all hell broke loose and aircraft were calling for recovery from all over the south-west of England. Controllers were frantically trying to identify and safely separate what appeared to be hundreds of tiny dots on the radar screen, all well mixed up with masses of glowing blobs of weather and other unwanted radar interference that covered the radar tube. As I stared, horrified, over the controller's shoulder, some sort of order slowly appeared out of the chaos. The aircraft moved and the blobs didn't. Four or more controllers were all talking at once, issuing orders to their assistants and instructions to their airborne customers. All too quickly, the little radar echoes converged on the airfield like homing bees, controllers conferred, sorting out the varying speeds and altitudes of the aircraft and, most importantly, their proximity to one another. As they entered the recovery pattern, each pilot requested, or demanded, some priority be given to his personal landing back at base. This was all heard over the speakers that were above each radar set and monitored the frequency on which that controller was operating. Eventually the aircraft were descended into a pattern of recovery that led, in the last phase, to a single controller in a ground controlled approach radar unit situated alongside the runway. It was his duty to guide the aircraft down to the last half mile or so when the pilot became visual with the runway and completed his own landing. With the last aircraft rolling down the runway, an exhausted silence pervaded the radar rooms and GCA truck on the airfield. The tension eased as adrenalin-filled controllers pushed their chairs back from the displays, wiped clean their annotated desk-tops and call signs, scribbled on and around the screen; trying to unwind before coping with the next recovery. With changes of staff, these operations went on from early morning until midnight or after, day after day. It crossed my mind that risking a heavy landing while flying, might have been the wiser choice after all.

RAF Shawbury was even more of an eye-opener. The ATC course provided a training that seemed to be a completely different art-form and from an earlier civilization. Some of the basics, of course, are fundamental, to provide safety and separation for aircraft on the ground and in the air. At Shawbury, the theory was practised in the classroom and in a mock up of a control tower visual control position, a large, glass-walled room at the top of the tower, inevitably called the VCP. Here, the task was to control ground movements on the airfield and in the airspace around the airfield on a single radio frequency. There was always constant liaison with the approach controllers in the darkened room below, working their several approach frequencies to bring airborne units to position where they could call the VCP for landing instructions. At Shawbury the approach system then consisted of, thankfully, an outdated system that used a radar-like tube that indicated a compass bearing to any aircraft calling on that particular frequency. The controller had no idea of the geographical position other than that the aircraft was somewhere on the bearing. With practice, or if your arithmetic was up to it, you could mentally add 180 degrees to the bearing on the tube. This provided a course to steer for the pilot to bring him overhead the air station. Once overhead, the recovery could be commenced by descending the aircraft out from the overhead in an approach pattern, timing the outbound leg to lose half the height and turning the aircraft inbound to close the airfield again to lose the remaining height and level off for safe approach to the airfield or a radar controlled landing.

If reading this has totally confused the reader, I can only say that they are well on the way to being air traffic controllers and that when they can bring four or more aircraft in to the airfield at the same time, they can qualify as I did. I relished my return to the relatively calmer chaos of a radar controlled approach pattern at Yeovilton, where one at least could see a presentation on the tube. I returned to my new duties with a far greater respect for air traffic controllers than I ever had as a pilot.

RNAS Yeovilton was the home of the Fleet Air Arm's disembarked night fighter squadrons. It was also the base used for the practical training for potential air direction controllers, whose role was to direct fighters, on ground radar, to engage enemy aircraft. They did this by night and by day using the Sea Venoms of a civilian contractor, as both 'ours' and 'theirs'. This, together with the day activities of the night fighters as they prepared for their night flying programmes, meant the airfield required the services of air traffic control for between sixteen and eighteen hours a day. I settled somewhat uneasily into the routines until called to attend the ground controllers approach course, also at Shawbury, later in the year. I found this course to be much more interesting. The radar was operated from a small caravan situated at the side of the runway. Manned by a single controller and with only a short range, it was designed to take control from the approach controllers in the tower and accurately feed each aircraft individually, by using its own, self-contained close-range traditional area radar display, showing an actual glide path pattern in both azimuth and elevation. The ground controller guided the pilot on his final descent, to within 100 feet above the ground and a quarter of a mile from the actual landing. The last few miles were under the total control of the controller on the ground. I think that because it was closer to my own flying experiences, I was more in my own element, with a one to one interaction, until you could say 'look ahead and land, GCA out', and seconds later came the diminishing roar of engines as the landing aircraft passed the van alongside the runway. The GCA, with its whirling radar on the roof, was invaluable when visibility was poor and, to keep both aircrew and controllers in constant practice, most landings at Yeovilton used a GCA approach.

I was always intrigued by the popular belief that the powerful magnetron, powering the radar in the GCA truck, and the massive radiation it emitted, was a sure fire contraceptive and that prolonged association would sterilize a man. There were often hopeful ratings hanging about outside when I took a breather and stepped outside.

True or not, my family, with only one child, has remained the same since those days, so the myth may well contain a grain of truth. I certainly spent my happiest air traffic control hours in the darkness of the interior, lit only by the eerie green glow of the radar tubes. As it was isolated from humdrum life in the tower, linked only by a phone and radio channels, it was not the most popular controller position, so there was little opposition when I volunteered to man the GCA.

After a year or so, with normal changes of staff caused by appointments to carriers and other duties, and by seniority, I became the senior watch keeping officer in the tower. This involved the supervision of the approach room operation, coordinating the various radar positions and generally maintaining the smooth running of the radar room. It was ironic that the duty meant I was no longer a watch keeper but worked daytime hours normally, overseeing all the watches in the tower.

After twelve months, my specialist flying pay was terminated. In itself it was a reasonable outcome as I was unlikely to fly again. However at the time there was provision for aircrew to take a two-year break from flying duties for a variety of reasons. There were many air traffic controllers who had availed themselves of this option so that their last years of service were ground based. There was naturally enough a proviso that they could be called back to flying duties if in an emergency, or there was a need to make up squadron numbers. I had never known of this occurring. I felt somewhat aggrieved that as I had been grounded through no fault of my own, while flying a prototype aircraft, testing it and other experimental equipment, I had suffered a substantial reduction in my salary. I realized that, if I had been advised, I could have taken such an option and completed my commission with another medical assessment if I extended my service.

I was not alone in my dismay; there were representations at the highest levels from serving senior officers, but to no avail. Our civilian masters were adamant and the decision was confirmed. As my twelve-year commission approached its end, I was confronted with a devil I did not know in civilian life and a devil I did know by continued employment in my present duties in the Navy. Over the last year or so, there had been several intimations that, if I applied for a permanent commission, it would be favourably accepted. As my terminal date drew nearer I made a decision and applied. Alas, in recent months there had been political change of policy and cutbacks in the Services were again in favour. Again the Navy had been forced to modify its plans to suit the ever-moveable goalposts. There was to be a concentration on helicopter operations with a phased reduction in fixed-wing aircraft. Air traffic controllers were no longer required and my application was turned down. As winter was approaching, I walked through the main gates of the airfield wearing my naval uniform for the last time.

After Christmas, the Royal Air Force delightedly accepted my offer to join them as an air traffic controller. They were under no budget restraints and desperate for experienced controllers. The wheel had turned full circle.

I was once again to become a new recruit in an armed service of Her Majesty, but this time in a uniform of a different shade of blue.

No mistaking me for the bus conductor this time.

Appendix

The Rules of Flying

1. Flying isn't dangerous. Crashing is.
2. Gravity is not just a good idea, it's a law. And it's not subject to appeal.
3. Every take-off is optional. Every landing is mandatory.
4. A 'good' landing is one from which you can walk away. A 'great' landing is one after which they can use the aircraft again.
5. Always try to keep the number of your landings equal to the number of your take-offs.
6. The probability of survival is inversely proportional to the angle of arrival.
7. You know you have landed with the wheels up when it takes full power to taxi back to dispersal.
8. It's always a good idea to keep the pointy end going forwards.
9. If you push the stick forward, the houses get bigger. If you pull it back they get smaller. Unless you pull it all the way back and hold it there. Then, after getting smaller they disappear, then reappear and start getting bigger again.
10. It's always better to be down here wishing you were up there, than up there wishing you were down here.
11. In the ongoing conflict between objects made of aluminium travelling at hundreds of miles an hour and the ground going at zero miles an hour, the ground has yet to lose.
12. Never let an aircraft take you to a place your brain didn't get to five minutes earlier.

13. The only time you have too much fuel is when you're on fire.

14. The propeller is just a big fan in front of the plane to keep the pilot cool. (If you don't believe this watch him sweat when it stops.)

15. When in doubt increase your altitude. No one has ever collided with the sky.

16. Stay out of clouds. The silver lining might be another aeroplane. Reliable sources also report that mountains have been known to hide in clouds.

17. Helicopters can't fly. They are just so ugly the Earth repels them.

18. Keep looking around. There's always something you've missed.

19. The three most useless things to a pilot are the altitude above you, the runway behind you and a tenth of a second ago.

20. Good judgment comes from experience. Unfortunately, experience usually comes from bad judgment.

21. You start with a bag full of luck and an empty bag of experience. The trick is to fill the bag of experience before you empty the bag of luck.

Index

1 Squadron 'A' Flight, 37
2 Squadron 'D' Flight, 41
700 Squadron, 150, 152
705 (helicopter) Squadron, 91, 118
737 Squadron, 50, 130, 134
751 Squadron, 83, 85
759 Squadron, 46
815 Squadron, x, 130,134, 137, 149
825 Squadron, 54, 57, 69

accident reports (A25), 99, 104, 125
accidents, 67, 82, 127, 128, 130, 139, 141, 143, 149, 162
Adden Atoll, 82
ADDLs, Lee-on-Solent, 89, 93
Allen, Brian
   and Maoris, 112
   and unexploded bomb, 140
   as Duty Aviation cadet, 17
   attends military funeral, 44
   birth of son, 127
   career and family, ix, 48, 96
   chewing gum hoax, 16
   commission, 7, 10
   fighter pilot training, 45, 49
   flying dual, 40
   flying training, 38, 3
   green parrot incident, 22
   helicopter roles, 48
   landing mirrors, 71
   landings, 47, 74
   married quarters, 59, 136, 137
   Mayday calls, 161
   missing shoes prank, 144
   on minesweeper, 25
   Purley Grammar School, 5
   rolling deck landings, 157
   rugby game, 113
   stopcock incident, 77
   straight deck batted landing, 86

tickler (tobacco allowance), 19
   training, 168
   water landing double ship, 103
   Whirlwind rescue, 104
   wings, 44
Allen, Patricia, viii, 137
Alvis engine, 121
anti-submarine warfare, 48
Argentina Naval Base, 116
Argentina, 115
Armstrong Siddeley works, 60, 61
assisted dummy-deck landings, 88
Auster, 79
Avro
   Lancaster, 51
   Shackleton, 50, 108
   Vulcan, 107

Baker, Lieutenant Doug, 46
batsman-controlled landings, 86
Bell helicopters, 115
Blackburn turbo-jet engine, 153
bolters, 73
bombs and bombing, 60, 69, 70
Bradley, Lieutenant Jim, 156
Bricker, Lieutenant Commander Gerry, 92, 114, 118
Buenos Aires, 116

catapult launch, 74, 75, 95
CENTO countries, 149
Chance-Vought Corsair (Whispering Death), 80
Chile, 115
Christmas Island, 100, 101
Clapham, 2
Colombo, 78
Cook Islands, 112
Cooper, Lieutenant John, 97
Cornabe, Lieutenant

Commander Knob, 138
Cornwall, 58, 59 132
Curtis, Midshipman Rick, 138, 141
Cyclone engines, 93
Daily Mail, 150
Dan-Air Troop charter, 137
Decca Navigation aid, 156
de Havilland
   Sea Venom, 74, 87, 138, 169
   Vampire, 22, 45, 46
discharged dead, 139
ditching, vii, 75, 135
Donegal, 129
Doodlebug alley, 3
Dorset, 133
Douglas Skyraider, 74

Egypt, 141
English Channel, 72
English Electric Canberra, 97, 98, 100, 107
Exercise Midlink 3, 149

Fairey
   Barracuda, 51
   Firefly, 50 ff
   Gannet A/S 1, 54, 69, 71
Falklands, 115
Far East, 71
Fleet Air Arm, vii
Flynn, Sub Lieutenant Bill, 148
formation flying, 4, 76
Fournel, Lieutenant Mike, 152

Galapagos Islands, 97
GCA (Ground Control Approach), 170
Gelder, RAN., Lieutenant Jim van, 69
Gibraltar, 20, 21, 76
goonsuits, 123
Greece, 141
Griffiths, 'Griff', 92
Grimes, Lieutenant Dennis, 99

Grumman Avenger (Turkey), 54, 86, 87, 104, 105, 114
Guest, Petty Officer, 11
Gurkhas, 79

Hampshire, 131
Harness, Leading Aircraftman, 123, 126, 128, 131
Hawaii, 99
Hawker Seahawk, 45, 49, 74, 82
H-bomb tests, 85, 100, 102
Hiller Helicopter, 120 ff
HMS
  Albion, ix. 74 79 ff, 137, 138, 139, 148, 150
  Bulwark, 72, 148
  Daedalus, (shore-based), 9, 83, 89
  Gannet, 50, 131
  Implacable, 17
  Impregnable, 28
  Melbourne, 50
  Ocean, 26
  Osprey, (shore-based), 131, 133, 164
  Royal Marquis, 28, 30
  Seahawk, (shore-based), 50, 56, 57
  Siskin (shore-based), 24, 121
  Tamar, 81
  Troubridge, 163
  Vernon, (shore-based), 25, 27
  Victorious, 149
  Warrior, (later Brazilian) 26, 83, 85, 86, 89, 91, 94, 103, 111, 117
Hong Kong, 78
Honolulu, 99
Hoot Owl (USN American Native rating), 147, 148
Hornchurch, 8
HRH Prince Philip, 119, 120

India, 77
Indian Navy, 78
Indian Ocean, 82
Isle of Wight, 3, 69, 72

Jamaica, 96
Japan, 143 ff
Johnson, Lieutenant Commander 'Johnny', 54, 61

Korea, 78, 143
Korean war, 50

La Fayette (French carrier), 79
lease-lend arrangements, 86
Lee-on-Solent, 83, 93, 118
Lister, Commissioned Pilot Tony, vii, ix, 3
Loch Foyle, 124

Magellan Straits, 115
Malacca Straits, 78
Malaya, 78
Malden (target) island, 85, 101, 108
Malta, 76, 137
McClure, Lieutenant Colin, 158, 159
Meadowcroft, Lieutenant Commander 'Porky', 125, 127, 128, 130
Minesweeper 1044, 152
Montevideo, 117
Moorcraft, Lieutenant Colin, 151
Morse code, 29
Mountbatten, Lord Louis, 139, 140

Nelson, Lord, 19
New Territories, Hong Kong, 81
Norman RN., Lieutenant Commander, 58
North American Harvard, 41

Operations
  Grapple, 85, 91, 92, 118
  Run Aground, 28, 30
  Starlight, 140

Panama Canal, 86, 94, 96
Patagonia, 115
Pearl Harbor, 99
Penrhyn Island, 111
Pensacola, 36, 37
Percival Prentice, 38, 41, 42
Perks, Sub Lieutenant Paul, 20
Peru, 11
Pitcairn Island, 111
Plant, Sub Lieutenant Johnny, 92
Port London, 101
Portland, 20, 133
Pratt and Whitney 'Wasp' radial engine, 121

RAE Bedford, 157
RAF Stations
  El Adem, 76

Lossiemouth, 45
Shawbury, 167
Syerston, 34, 44
Watton, 83, 87, 88, 89
Rayment, Lieutenant Mike, 145
Reid, Lieutenant Dick, 76
Richardson, Lieutenant Commander Sid, 87
River Plate, 117
RNAS
  Eglinton, N.Ireland, 4, 121, 127, 131
  Yeovilton, x, 150, 158, 169

Saunders Roe P531 helicopter, 153, 155
Scotland, 47
Sikorsky
  Dragonfly, 121, 128
  Whirlwind, 86, 121, 156
Sinclair, Lieutenant Commander 'Sandy', 53
Singapore, 78
Southsea, 28
Spreadbury, Lieutenant Commander Ted, 119
sproule net, 122
Stretton base, Manchester, 48
Suez Canal, 141

Thatcher, Lieutenant Cowan, 99
The Death of Nelson (painting), 164
The Girl Mary, 129
The Royal Yacht Britannia, 31, 32, 33
Tobruk, 139
trolleyac system, 39
Turkey, 98

Valparaiso, 115
Victory in Europe, 3
Vikrant Indian navy, vii, 78

Wailes, Lieutenant Jeremy R. de B., 125
Wakeford, Lieutenant Brian, 137
Westland
  Sea King, 143
  Wessex, 143
Williams, Lieutenant John, 92
Wilson, Sub Lieutenant Tony, ix, 130, 131, 137, 142, 150
Wright radial Cyclone engine, 86, 97